The Sweetest Song

Other books by Richard Wurmbrand

Answer to Moscow's Bible
Christ on the Jewish Road
If that were Christ, would you give him your blanket?
If Prison Walls Could Speak
In God's Underground
Little Notes That Like Each Other
One Hundred Prison Meditations
Reaching Towards the Heights
Sermons in Solitary Confinement
Stronger than Prison Walls
The Underground Saints
The Wurmbrand Letters
Tortured for Christ
Was Marx a Satanist?
Where Christ is Tortured
Where Christ Still Suffers
Marx: Prophet of Darkness

The Song of Solomon expressed through the lives of saints and martyrs

Richard Wurmbrand

Marshall Morgan and Scott
Marshall Pickering
1 Beggarwood Lane, Basingtoke, Hants RG23, 7LP, UK

Copyright © 1988 R. Wurmbrand
First published in 1988 by Marshall Morgan and Scott Publications Ltd
Part of the Marshall Pickering Holdings Group
A subsidiary of the Zondervan Corporation

All rights reserved. No part of this publication may be reproduced, stored in a retrieval system, or transmitted, in any form or by any means, electronic, mechanical, photocopying, recording or otherwise, without the prior permission in writing, of the publisher

British Library CIP Data

Wurmbrand, Richard
  The sweetest song.
  1. Bible. O.T. Song of Solomon – Texts
  with commentaries
  I. Title
  223'.906

  ISBN 0-551-01652-3

Text Set in Baskerville by Brian Robinson, Buckingham
Printed in Great Britain by Cox and Wyman, Reading

≈ Contents ≈

Introduction	7
Chapter 1	17
Chapter 2	76
Chapter 3	121
Chapter 4	137
Chapter 5	160
Chapter 6	174
Chapter 7	191
Chapter 8	201
Last Considerations	218
References	223

≈ Introduction ≈

In *Zohar* (The Light), main book of the Kabbalah, a work which contains the Jewish mystical tradition, it is written:

> The Song of Songs is superior to all songs that preceded it, for those which were sung by Solomon's predecessors ascended only to join with the songs chanted by the company of angels; as for instance, the 'Song of Degrees to David' [the literal translation of the Hebrew *le David*], which means 'The song which celestial grades sing to David' to solicit nourishment from him . . . But when Solomon came, he sang a song that is higher even than David's song, one that is the very same as that sung by the great ones of the realms above, the pillars of the universe, in honour of the Supernal King who is the Lord in all peace and harmony. Other men send up praises by means of lower chariots, but King Solomon by means of higher chariots . . .
>
> On the day when this song was revealed the *Shekinah* (God's glory) descended to earth, as it is written, 'And the priests could not stand to minister because of the cloud.' Why? Because 'the glory of the Lord had filled the house of the Lord' (1 Kings 8:11). On that day this hymn was revealed, and Solomon sang this song in the power of the Holy Spirit, wherein is to be found the summary of the whole Law of Moses, the whole work of creation, the mystery of the Patriarchs, the story of the Egyptian exile, and the Exodus therefrom, and the Song of the Sea. It is the quintessence of the Decalogue, of the Sinaitic covenant, of the significance of Israel's

wanderings through the desert until their arrival in the Promised Land and the building of the Temple. It contains the crowning of the Holy Name with love and joy, the prophecy of Israel's exile among the nations, of their redemption, of the resurrection of the dead, and all else until that day which is 'Sabbath to the Lord'. All that was, and shall be, is contained in it; and, indeed, even that which will take place on the 'Seventh Day', which will be the 'Lord's Sabbath', is indicated in this song.

It is a song in which those who are above and those who are below participate; a song formed in the likeness of the world above, which is the supernal Sabbath, a song through which the supernal Holy Name is crowned. Therefore it is holy of holies. Why so? Because all its words are full of love and joy.

In the *Babylonian Talmud* (another sacred book of the Jewish people) the following words spoken by Rabbi Akiba are recorded: 'No day in the history of the world is so precious as the day on which the Song of Songs was given to Israel; for all the other Scriptures are holy, but the Song of Songs is holiest of all.' By the same token, we could say that the lives of all those who really deserve the name of 'Christian' are holy. We are all sanctified by faith, by the blood shed for us, because that blood was Divine. But there are lives which are holiest of all – the lives of the persecuted Church, the lives of those who suffer in jail or in psychiatric asylums, in chains and in hunger, deprived of their loved ones, because they follow faithfully in the footsteps of the Master.

This book will be a kind of commentary upon Solomon's Song. It will be a unique commentary – or rather, a new translation of the Song. It will be a translation of it into the lives of saints and martyrs, most of them from our own times, who belong to the Underground Church in the Communist countries.

The decision about which Jewish books should be included in, and which excluded from the Old Testament was taken by the Synod of Iabne. The Synod debated very heatedly over the inclusion of the Song of Songs as a sacred book. It was accused of being a worldly book, because it spoke with simplicity about love between a man and woman, and sometimes it employed sexual imagery. But in the end the Song's opponents were overruled.

In this book, as in many other parts of the Bible, the images of relationships such as those between bridegroom and bride are only poetic devices to represent the union of the believing soul and God, of the chosen people and their Master. The author of Solomon's Song is a mystic: he expresses himself in the normal language of mysticism.

If the inclusion of the Song in the Bible was a matter for heated debate, it is no wonder that the Underground Church in Communist countries is also hotly debated. Some prelates and theologians consider it to be a bunch of fanatics without any justification.

It is alleged that those who are imprisoned for Christ's sake in Communist countries suffer from masochistic tendencies, that they want to suffer, that they have a 'martyr complex'. It is said that they are not reasonable. They refuse to make the compromise demanded by life and by a dictatorship – compromises which would result in liberty to worship within the limits prescribed by the atheist government.

Not all souls are the same. Some rivers flow quietly between their banks; others overflow. There exist choice souls, whose love of God cannot be confined to the narrow limits of what is considered a normal faith. Their cup runs over. Their love of God burns.

Solomon's Song answers to the desires of such hearts. Only men such as these are found in the Underground Church.

Rabia of Basra, a Moslem mystic, used to pray: 'O Lord, in public I invoke You in the way one invokes his master. In public I say, 'O my God,' but when we are alone I say, 'O my Beloved.' She also said: 'O Lord, if I adore You because I fear hell, let me burn in hell; and if I adore You because I hope for paradise, exclude me from paradise. But if I adore You for what You Yourself are, do not deprive me of the vision of Your eternal beauty.' She said to God, 'I do not desire from You either this world or the one to come. You are enough for me.'

Solomon's Song is written for such hearts. It is a poem of love between Israel and his Saviour.

Spiritual greed

There is a burning spiritual desire which might well be called 'spiritual greed' by sceptics, because it is outwardly very similar to fleshly greed.

A beggar once said to an emperor who wished to give him charity, 'Give me anything you like; but I will impose a condition.'

The emperor was intrigued. He had never met such a beggar. 'And what is that condition?' he asked.

'You must fill my bowl up completely.'

The emperor laughed. 'I can certainly do that,' he replied. 'I can even fill your bowl with diamonds!'

He called for diamonds to be poured into the beggar's bowl. As they fell in, they disappeared.

The emperor roared in fury. 'I will not be shamed by this beggar, even if my whole kingdom disappears!'

But no precious stones that were poured into the bowl ever stayed there; they always disappeared.

Finally the emperor swallowed his pride and asked the beggar to tell him the secret of the bowl.

'It is made out of human selfishness,' he explained. 'It covets all things, yet it remains always empty, always hungry, never satisfied.'

Luxurious cars, big bank accounts, fine houses, high position and reputation – they are only challenges to the ego, serving only to whet its appetite for more. This, then is fleshly greed.

Spiritual greed exists too. Some of the disciples asked Jesus, 'Grant unto us that we may sit, one on Your right hand, and the other on Your left, in Your glory' (Mark 10:37). They did not know what they were asking for.

In spiritual matters, the only real glory is in the renunciation of glory. The jewels of personal glory and self-aggrandizement will be swallowed up by the beggar's bowl, even if they are jewels of the spirit. The bowl is never satisfied. It is never filled.

Solomon's Song belongs to those who have made the greatest renunciation of all: the renunciation of themselves. For them, only the Beloved counts.

Singing the Jesus Song

The famous pianist Rubinstein was in the company of a large number of music-lovers who were discussing the works of Chopin. One of them asked, 'How would Chopin himself have played his compositions?' Rubinstein sat down at the piano and began to play. When he finished, there were tears in his listeners' eyes as they said, 'Now we have heard Chopin himself.'

Comment upon what King Solomon sang to the praise of the Saviour in his rare moments of spiritual exultation must be made in the same state of the spirit as Solomon's when he composed his Song. When reading a commentary upon the Song of Songs, the reader should feel that he has heard Solomon himself at his best.

It is said that when David was a young boy at the court of King Saul, he asked permission to play on a beautiful harp that was lying unused in the throneroom. The king said, 'It's useless – I have been cheated. I paid a great deal for that harp, because it was spoken of highly. But the best harpists have tried it, and it was painful to hear the ugly sounds it produced. It's the worst harp that you could imagine.'

But David persisted, and because the king loved him greatly, permission was granted. When he played, the music was so beautiful that when it ended, all the court wept. They had been moved to the depths of their hearts.

'How is it,' demanded the king, 'that so many tried to play this harp, and only you succeeded?'

David replied, 'All the others tried to play their own songs, and the harp refused to yield to their wishes. I played to the harp its own song. You saw its joy when I reminded it of the days when it was a young tree in the forest. I told it about sunbeams playing in its branches, about chirping birds, and about lovers embracing each other in its shadow. The harp was glad to remember those days.

'Then I told the story of the evil men who came and felled the innocent tree. It was a sad day. Its life as a tree had finished. But I told the harp that death cannot triumph over life. The tree has died as a tree, but its wood has become a harp which can sing forever the glories of the eternal God. And the harp, which had wept when I told about her death, now rejoiced, made jubilant again.

'When the Messiah comes, many will try to play their own songs on his harp. The results will be tragically dissonant. On the Messiah's harp, you must play his own song – the song of his eternal glory with God, the song of his humiliation as a babe in a manger, the song of a life in sorrow, opposition and poverty on earth, the song of his being whipped and crucified and buried. But then also the song of his resurrection, ascension and enthronement in heaven.

'Then the harp will give a beautiful sound. Then his congregation will shine like a sun.'

In writing this book, I have no song of my own to sing. I sing the Song of Jesus and of His bride as Solomon sang it; and to make the song resound more beautifully than ever, I illustrate it with lives of saints and martyrs. Let us sing for him with the same burning love and adoration with which the angels sang in Bethlehem at Jesus' birth.

A great sinner's song

There is something remarkable in the title of the book, The Song of Songs which is Solomon's. God arranged that the holiest book of the Bible should be written by one of its worst characters.

There was much that was positive in King Solomon's reign over Israel. He secured the nation a long period of peace, but in his personal life he was beneath contempt.

He had a large number of wives and concubines. Every one of them lived in palaces and was provided with luxuries. He indulged in all the pleasures which fleshly life can provide. This cost enormous amounts of money which had to be raised by slave labour. He frequently flogged men into complying with the demands of his debauchery.

In the light of all this, many theologians have expressed doubts as to whether Solomon has any part in God's salvation. Happily, God does not always agree with the theologians: he saves whom he wishes. Salvation is all by grace and condescension. To demonstrate this, he gave the inspiration to write his most beautiful book to one whose moral achievements were very few.

Miracles are signs of the presence of God. Divine inspiration of this book is proved by the miracle that such a bad man wrote it. You would not have thought he was capable of it. The only man we know for sure is in paradise (because Jesus confirmed it) is a man who had been a robber all of his adult life and only in his very last moments said a few words expressing faith. One of the foremost apostles, Saint Paul, had been a murderer. Mary Magdalene had been a loose woman. One of the most moral and profound of love stories, *The happy prince*, was written by Oscar Wilde, a man convicted for debauchery. There are many other similar instances. So we should not be surprised that the most beautiful song in the Bible was composed by a great sinner.

Think of Richard Wagner. He is described as ungrateful in love and irresponsible in politics. He was conceited and suffered from senile erotomania; he was also a fierce anti-Semite. But this in no way diminishes the value of his music.

We must learn to distinguish the value of a work from the value of the man who is behind it. The fact is that God sometimes uses very bad men for very good deeds, and that sometimes very good men do poor work.

All the 'types' or foreshadowings of Jesus in the Old Testament were men who had committed many bad deeds. We could not expect it to be otherwise; the type is always inferior to the typified.

Only one thing counts

One of the greatest accusations of the Soviet press against the Underground Church is that many of its leaders are former thieves, murderers and even war criminals whose hands are stained with blood. This would not discredit those church leaders in our sight, even if the things being said against them were true.

The Russian poet, Tiutchev, wrote: 'You can't understand Russia with your mind. You can't measure it with the usual yardstick. Russia is something unique; you can only have confidence in it.' These words are even truer when applied to the most beautiful part of the Russian nation – its Christians gathered in the Underground Church.

Where unique events happen, as in biblical times, very bad characters can be inspired with the most beautiful thoughts; robbers and murderers become illustrious saints. The children of God can rejoice about this.

The following is one of the oldest sermon illustrations used in the Christian Church. It is also a good test of one's understanding of what Christianity is about.

There once lived a dwarf who was also a hunchback and very, very ugly. Nobody ever invited him to a party; nobody showed him love, or even attention. He became disillusioned with life and decided to climb a mountain and throw himself from its peak into the abyss.

When he ascended the mountain, he met a very beautiful girl. He talked to her and discovered that she was climbing the mountain for the same purpose. Her suffering was at the other extreme. She had everybody's attention and love, but the one whom she loved and who had loved her too had forsaken her for another girl, because the other was rich. She felt life had no meaning for her any more. They decided to make the ascent together.

While they continued to climb, they met a man who introduced himself as a police officer in search of a very dangerous bandit who had robbed and murdered many people. The king had promised a large reward to the person who captured him. The police officer was very confident: 'I will catch him because I know he has a feature by which he can be recognised. He has six fingers on his right hand. The police have been looking for him for years. For the last two or three, nothing has been heard from him, but he has to pay for a multitude of crimes in the past.'

The three climbed the mountain. Near its peak was a monastery. Its abbot, although he had become a monk only recently, had quickly attained great renown for saintliness. When they entered the monastery, he came to meet them. You could see the glory of God in his face. As the girl bowed to kiss his right hand, she saw he had six fingers. With this, the story ends.

Those who hear this story are perplexed; it can't finish like this! What happened to the dwarf, the girl, the policeman; and was the criminal caught?

The beauty of the story is that it does finish here. Something beautiful has happened: a criminal hunted because of his many robberies and murders has become a great saint, renowned for his godly life. All the rest is of no further interest. The great miracle has been performed. Christ has been born in the heart of a man of very low character.

The Hebrew language has no superlative. It says 'vanity of vanities' for 'the most worthless vanity' or 'the heaven of heavens' for 'the highest heaven.' With God everything is possible: the Song of Songs (which means in Hebrew, 'the superlative song') is written by a superlative sinner.

Because of this, the heights of Solomon's song are accessible to every one of us, whatever our past has been, and however deep we may have fallen in sin.

≈ *Chapter 1* ≈

Only his kiss

The bride says, 'Let him kiss me with the kisses of his mouth: for your love is better than wine' (1:2).

The *Zohar* says that at Mount Sinai, when the Law was given, every individual Israelite was asked by God if he would accept him and all his commandments, to which the reply came, 'Yes.' He was asked again, 'Will you accept me and all the penalties attached to my Law?' And again he answered, 'Yes.' Then he was kissed on the mouth. Similarly, the bride in Solomon's Song says, 'Let him kiss me with the kisses of his mouth.' The *Zohar* continues:

'No other love is like unto the ecstasy of the moment when spirit cleaves to spirit in a kiss, more especially a kiss on the mouth, which is the well of the spirit and its medium. When mouth meets mouth, spirits unite one with the other and become one – one love.'

The Hebrew word for 'love' is written *A H B H*. The *Zohar* says, 'First comes the letter *Aleph* (our A). Then comes the letter H which unites itself with the *Aleph* in love. From these two other letters issue and spirits are interlocked with spirits of love.'

Let us compare these words with the boring, prosaic, annoying prayers which we say usually and we will realise the distance between us and the soul enamoured with God – a soul which has a burning love like that of the ideal bride. She knows no peace nor rest until she finds God himself. Every other being, every other thing, only increases her desire, her thirst to see him. She is never satisfied with anybody or anything except himself. She has drunk enough of the water of this world and she has remained thirsty. Now she desires him, saying: 'Let *him* kiss me with the kisses of *his* mouth.'

A believer is attached to his spiritual leader – to his pastor. But if the pastor is aware of his responsibilities, he must strive to make the believer more and more independent of him. A psychiatrist, having solved the complexes of his patient, has a duty to free him also from the complex of dependence upon the physician which has arisen during the treatment.

A pastor must be like a matchmaker, who persuades a girl to marry somebody else. He must be very careful that the girl does not fall in love with himself, the matchmaker. The pastor must be a guide enabling the believer to reach the bridegroom. He must ignite a love for the bridegroom in the hearts of the believers, so that after hearing one of his sermons the congregation should not say, 'How beautifully he has preached' but 'How wonderful Jesus is!' Remaining attached to the pastor and not passing through him to the Saviour about whom he preaches can be a deadly danger for the believer. Pastors are men and have all the temptations of men. Some of them are very, very weak.

The movement called 'Christian Endeavour' within the reformed churches is forbidden in Communist Rumania, but exists underground. A girl belonging to this movement was beaten and tortured to force her to make accusing statements against her pastor. She remained faithful to Christ and refused. But to her surprise, when she was brought before a court that same pastor came as a prosecution witness against her. He had yielded to pressure without much resistance. His testimony against her contributed to her being sentenced, but her love for Christ did not depend upon the attitudes and behaviour of the pastor who had brought her to salvation. She had been freed from that attachment to him. She continued to remain faithful, and she never said one bitter word about the pastor who had been so treacherous.

This was a soul who had a right to receive the kisses of Jesus himself. When you are in his embrace, disappointments with pastors don't count anymore. The soul which burns with love for Christ is not satisfied with his messengers, even his finest messengers. They don't answer the deep need of the soul. Their presence serves only to irritate. The duty of a pastor is only to reveal to men how unhappy they are without Jesus. Then he must tell them how he has found Jesus, and how they can find him too.

For the bride, the simple fact that she is surrounded by messengers of the bridegroom is a proof of the sad fact that the bridegroom himself is absent. She desires him, only him. None of his messengers can adequately represent him. None of them can take his place. The most gifted preachers can only stutter about him. She has one desire: 'Let him kiss me with the kisses of his mouth.' She longs for him, and yearns that his presence should show itself through a kiss. In biblical times people kissed the hand of the king, and even this was considered a privilege. Until quite recently, everyone who approached the Pope had to kiss his foot. The faithful Christian soul desires a kiss from Jesus' mouth.

The relationship between God and the faithful soul is really like the relationship between a bridegroom and a bride. Both desire kisses. The heavenly Father, who knows the desires of Jesus, in Psalm 2:12 commands us to 'Kiss the Son.' Jesus reproves a Pharisee, telling him, 'You gave me no kiss' (Luke 7:45). He could make this reproach to many of us. We gave him many words; we gave him our energy and our time; we put our money in the collection boxes of the church. But we did not give him the one, supreme thing for which he longs – a kiss. The faithful soul's desire is the same as his. She sighs, 'Let him kiss me with the kisses of his mouth.'

This reciprocal desire has been frequently satisfied. Mary Magdalene kissed the feet of Jesus. After her, many penitents have done likewise, and many prodigal sons who have returned to the Father have seen him coming to meet them, embracing them and kissing them repeatedly.

Only those who have ever received such a kiss can know the sweetness of Jesus. Only the person who has humbled himself for his sins or entrusted himself to God in great dangers can say how dear are his promises: that now there is peace between him and God, that God loves him and will protect him.

We have to be careful that the kiss should be Jesus' kiss. Souls in sorrow seek comfort, and accept it readily from wherever it comes. But not so the true Bride of Christ. There is only one object of her love. She does not even consider it necessary to say whose kisses she receives. She doesn't name him. For example, Mary Magdalene, seeing the empty tomb of Jesus, tells the man whom she supposed to be the gardener, 'They have taken away my Lord, and I know not where they have laid him.' (John 20:13). Who is the Lord about whom she speaks? Does she have to pronounce his name? She thinks that only one can be 'the Lord.'

For the Bride, only one person exists. She assumes that others feel the same. She does not profane the Holy Name by pronouncing it too often. The elect of God will understand. The Beloved can't be anybody else but Jesus.

Young brides

Souls who have such an intimate knowledge of Jesus

adopt unique attitudes. One such soul is Leonas Sileikis. When a seventh grade pupil at school, he was summoned to a meeting of the school administration where his faith was to be considered. Leonas' father came to the meeting uninvited. Leonas was asked whether he had read the atheistic books his teacher had given him. He had – six of them in all.

'What do you think of these books?' they asked him.

'They're lies and slander,' Leonas replied.

After a long discourse against religion, the teacher, Miss Misiuniene, asked Leonas, 'Do you renounce your faith?'

'I believe, and I will continue to believe,' was the reply.

The teacher then explained to the father how religion supposedly damages children. 'Nowadays, very few people go to church, so one must go along with the majority', she said.

To this, Leonas replied, 'Only a dead body is carried along with the current. A live person can always swim against the stream.'

Leonas will have to suffer for his faith. But he has known the kiss of Jesus, and so the adversity of the world does not count for him.

In Rumania, you cannot study in a university without being a member of the Communist youth organisation. You must render lipservice to its God-hating doctrines. Lydia C. had been the first in all grades of high school. Now a university education was guaranteed. As an exceptional student she would also receive an allowance for her further education. She had only to deliver a speech at the inauguration of the year of study. The big shots of the Communist Party were there.

She praised Communism, all right. She got great applause. But she finished with the words: 'These things one has to say, if you wish to advance in our society. But I don't believe one word of what I just said. I believe in God and will follow him.'

With this, she had ruined her whole future. Instead of becoming a doctor as she had desired, she became a seamstress. But souls who have received Jesus' kiss cannot compromise. They can praise only him.

Where can you get his kiss?

It is not difficult to receive his kiss. This was no problem for the Virgin Mary. Her Saviour was her obedient child. She could receive his caresses whenever she desired. Mary Magdalene and even Judas could kiss him. And there is no doubt that he reciprocated their kisses.

Christ lives with every believer as much as he lived in his mother's home, (though as a diamond yet unearthed, enclosed within the ground), because we are his image, members of his body. The Virgin Mary kissed Jesus' lips, and his hair, his hands and his breast. She could kiss his physical body. But Jesus is the only person who has two bodies: that of the Jewish carpenter who lived 2,000 years ago, which is seated now in heaven, and that of the Church. So we can kiss him when we kiss our brothers and sisters, and in the same way we can receive his kisses.

Jesus said, 'Blessed are the pure in heart: for they shall see God' (Matthew 5:8). They will see him not only in the next world. They will see him in every brother – yes, in every human being. Those who sentenced to death St Stephen, the first martyr of Christianity, 'looking steadfastly on him, saw his face as it had been the face of an angel' (Acts 6:15). They could see the angel in their victim. Let us at least learn from them how to look upon our brethren. Then we will be able to receive as many holy kisses as the Virgin Mary was able to obtain from Jesus.

Jesus taught also that anyone who feeds the hungry,

gives drink to the thirsty, takes in strangers, clothes the naked or visits the sick and the prisoners does this to him (Matthew 25:35-40). He identifies himself with the sufferers. The kiss of a person starving, oppressed or longing after love is his kiss.

For example, I know of a Christian prisoner in a Communist prison camp. He was near to death; his wasted body lay on the floor. Then he saw what seemed to be a girl bathed in glory. She looked like a nun. In her hand she held the living bread, and put it to his parched mouth. I know, too, of a sister in the USA. She had a vision in which she saw herself in a Communist prison, putting bread to a prisoner's mouth.

No walls separate the persecuted Church from that which enjoys freedom. The most amazing letter I ever received came from Canada. It was from a man who had been in jail for robbery. As a punishment for misbehaviour he had been put into solitary confinement. There he sought God, but had difficulty finding him. Then he heard an inner voice speaking to him, comforting him and giving him counsel. He was converted. Once out of jail, he joined a church. In a bookshop he found a book that caught his interest. It was my book, *Sermons in Solitary Confinement*. He recognised the sermons. It had been my voice that had spoken to him. We had been in solitary confinement at the same time – he in Canada, I in Rumania. Angels carried my words to him. Prison walls, two continents and an ocean had been no barriers to them.

The kisses of his glorified body

The Bride desires Jesus' kisses. She wants her mouth to be touched. Jeremiah says, 'The Lord put forth his hand and touched my mouth' (Jeremiah 1:9). Isaiah says, 'Then flew one of the seraphims unto me, having a live coal in his hand, which he had taken with the tongs from off the altar:

and he laid it upon my mouth' (Isaiah 6:6–7). Thus the iniquity of Isaiah was removed. The church fathers saw in this burning coal a symbol of the Son of God incarnate. In Christian Syriac poetry, Jesus is called *Kemurta Denura*, which means 'the burning coal.' He must touch our lips, so that we can praise him with fire.

I can be kissed by those who belong to his body on earth, but is it possible to kiss Jesus who is in heaven? Can the lips of his glorified body touch our lips? How can I know if my prayer has been heard? How can I know if I have received that kiss which I desire?

Some prominent saints have had this privilege. Saint Anthony held Jesus at his breast. According to a legend, Hermann Joseph presented an apple to an image of the child Jesus; Jesus put aside his sceptre, descended from the image and took the apple.

Henry Suso asked the Virgin Mary to show him the baby and to allow him to kiss Jesus. He took Jesus into his arms; he held in his arms the small baby who is bigger than the universe. One minute of such an experience transforms wolves into meek men, angry people into quiet people, the proud into the humble.

To St Mechtild, Henry's sister, the Child said, 'When I was born into the world I was immediately wrapped in swaddling clothes in which I could not move; it demonstrated that I and all that I brought with me have been given into the hands of men, who may dispose of us as they wish. The bound man has no might. He cannot defend himself. You can take from him what he has. When I left the world I was nailed to a cross. I could not move. It was a sign that I left all men the good I had done for them.'

Saint Birgit of Sweden saw Jesus' birth. He was born painlessly, in a moment, looking towards the east, while the Virgin knelt in prayer. He lay naked and shining on the ground, more radiant than the sun. When Mary realised that he was born, she adored the child with great reverence. 'Welcome, my Lord and my son,' she said.

Therese of Lisieux became Jesus' toy. Charles de Foucauld received at Bethlehem the illuminating revelation that he ought always to take the least significant place, in order to be small and helpless like his Master at his birth.

But what should we others do, who are not capable of such mystic elevations?

Sanctified imagination

We all know the plague of erotic fantasies. In prison, sexual obsession is one of the greatest sufferings of saints, especially the younger ones. Many of them never saw their girlfriends or their wives. I myself saw virtually no women or girls for fourteen years. You sat on concrete in a common cell with hands on knees, and you were forbidden to move. You never had a book; you were not allowed to speak, even whisper, to your cellmate; sometimes you were on your own; you could do nothing but fantasize or think. For hours, erotic images paraded before the Christians' eyes. The more they were suppressed, the more powerful they became.

Sometimes the Communist jails are very refined. They used to parade girls in miniskirts in front of the sexually hungry prisoners. They took prisoners to the beaches and showed them girls in bikinis. They told them, 'This is what you can have if you deny your faith.'

When Milan Haimovici, a Rumanian Hebrew Christian pastor, was in prison they brought a prostitute into his solitary cell and forced him to share his bed with her, night after night, when for years he had been isolated from the world. The wardens spied through the peephole, watching to see if anything happened. They had cameras ready to photograph him embracing her, so that they could disgrace him.

Girls or men whom you see only in your imagination, when you kiss, embrace or mate in your sexual fantasy, might not be physically present, but they are very real – so real that they can drive you mad.

The only defence against erotic obsession is to spiritualise it, to see in every erotic image (as Solomon teaches us) an image of our intimate love as brides of Christ for our Bridegroom. Everybody can become a bride of Christ, through faith. A male who is converted becomes not a bridegroom, but a bride. (It was Jung who identified a female element in men which he called the *anima*, just as in women there is a male element, the *animus*). Through assiduous spiritual exercises we can train our imaginations. We can adopt the posture of the bride longing for the Bridegroom, desiring and receiving the kisses of the holy Lover and finding our full joy in him. Like many other visions of the saints, this can become a spiritual reality in our lives. By dreaming about an ardent union of his soul with Jesus, Pastor Milan Haimovici overcame the temptations of the prostitute.

Souls who know the spiritual realities no more doubt such kisses than one doubts a kiss received from an earthly lover.

Saint Therese of Avila writes, 'As those who love each other do not allow themselves to be disturbed, those who have received this kiss despise all the things of the world, according them very small worth. Having seen the vanity of material things they despise them.' The person who has received the kiss knows he has received it. Then he desires to be kissed more and more, and to be left undisturbed by anybody or anything, in sweet fellowship with Jesus.

Don't try to fight erotic fantasies head-on. Use the expulsive power of sanctified imagination. You can't stop a little girl playing with dolls. No educator's theories can achieve that. But there comes a time when the girl grows up. She acquires new interests, and these displace from her heart the pleasure of playing with dolls. In the same way, if you let sexual imaginings alone, and if every moment you are free of them you cultivate more and more spiritual imaginings, in time the spiritual fantasy will expel the mind's erotic obsessions.

In *Nash Sovremennik*, a Soviet magazine, the writer J. Kasakov wrote in 1977 that he sometimes observed his baby smiling in his dreams. His mother interpreted this to mean that angels were playing with the child. (They were Communists, who had not been taught about angels.) Kasakov wrote, 'What is the smile? What does a babe know that is concealed from grown-ups?'

Another Soviet writer, L. Vorobiov, tells of a father and daughter eating in a monastery in Russia, which the Communists had transformed into a restaurant. The daughter said reproachfully, 'We drink beer and become gluttons, where once monks ate their meals in piety.'

The father replied that the monks also drank.

She upbraided him for condemning monks for hypocrisy, when the Communists today were no better. Then she told him that she wanted to enter a convent.

'I suggest that you read some pornography,' he answered.

'I have,' she said. 'I am bored by it.'

On the way back home, travelling by boat, the father had a mystical experience in which he saw the golden cupola of a cathedral advancing towards him. This happened in 1976 in Moscow.

If the Communists can spontaneously experience spiritual imaginings, how much more can the bride of Christ, versed in Scripture, consciously bring before her imagination the heavenly things. She can rejoice in them with jubilation, and expel much of the harm of erotic fantasies.

I will not, however, gloss over one difficulty. Many who, over decades of imprisonment, have conquered erotic obsessions, cannot so easily master themselves when, freed, they see real females again. It is the same for

Christian women when they were released. Instincts, long restrained, took their revenge. Even with the best of brides, the struggle never ends. But they can be finally victorious, if they never give up. They can come to rejoice in the embraces of Christ.

The mouth which is covered by kisses only momentarily breaks free to speak words of love to the beloved, which will indicate more kissing. When one has received the heavenly kiss of unspeakable sweetness one falls silent. One lady for years told everybody about her experiences with Jesus. Then one day she had a real experience with him. From that time on, she kept quiet. Sometimes those who receive the heavenly kiss do not know the Bible well, and cannot speak in biblical language; but they too can know the Bridegroom's embraces.

The Christian Mission to the Communist World has often been threatened by terrorists. Its Swiss branch, called 'Relief Action for the Martyr Church', received a threatening letter from a group called the Red Army Faction. The Swiss Christians remained unafraid and continued their work, for which they were rewarded by the Lord. One day they received a letter from a terrorist. 'I had an experience with Jesus and hesitate between terrorism and God,' it read. 'I am out of balance, please advise.' Anyone who has been kissed by someone previously unknown but very lovable will know how he felt.

The Christians established contact with him immediately. Soon they received a second letter: 'Since the age of seventeen I have been a terrorist. Now I have surrendered my heart to Christ. It was terrible when I realised how huge my sins were; they were higher than the Himalayas. I was also an adorer of Satan. Now I would not like to be the sort of Christian who only prays a little and reads the Bible rarely, but rather a fighter in the front line.'

His two natures

'Let him kiss me with the kisses of his mouth,' says the bride at the beginning of Solomon's Song, 'for your love is better than wine.' It is as if the bride is speaking about two different persons: 'Let *him* kiss me . . . for *your* love . . .' The bride is thinking about the two natures which combine in the person of Jesus – the human nature and the divine.

The love of Jesus' human nature is better than wine, better than all the pleasures this world can offer. But the bride wants more. She wishes to see the glorified Son of God in all his splendour, and she desires the kisses of his divine nature.

Some Christians' lives and deaths are far more painful than our own. Equatorial Guinea was for many years under the oppression of the dictator Macias Nguema, who was supported by Soviet, Cuban and East German advisers. At the time, refugees fleeing to Gabon from there told of thirty-six Christians who were buried up to the neck in the forest. The next day only two heads were still moving. They were disfigured by insect bites and the eyes had been eaten. In another incident, a prisoner had his feet hacked off; in another, a girl who refused the sexual advances made by her guards was tortured unspeakably with a burning torch.[1]

Lukewarm Christians cannot endure such things. The privilege of bearing such a heavy cross and remaining faithful and hopeful is the monopoly of those who have received the holy kiss of his divine nature, though they may not have thought about or even heard of this biblical phrase.

Bonaventure was the first Superior of the Franciscan Order after the death of its founder. He was once asked by Saint Thomas Aquinas where all his extensive knowledge came from. He pointed to the crucifix on his desk. 'That is the source of all my knowledge,' he said. 'I study only Jesus Christ, and him crucified.' Bonaventure had received the holy kiss of the divine nature of Jesus.

The savour of his ointments

In the Orient, perfumed wood was sometimes used in the building of mosques. It is like hearing sermons preached in a church in which incense is burned or in one decorated with sweet-smelling flowers. But I have heard the Word preached or recited in Communist prison cells, in which sometimes 200 prisoners were crammed together, in indescribable squalor. Some of us were unable to wash for years. Our clothes were filthy. Water was scarce, and so was soap. Overflowing barrels in the cell served as lavatories for 200 people. Faeces and urine filled one corner. Many of the prisoners simply suffocated. The windows were shuttered so that air could not enter. Men would lie down on the floor so as to breathe the draught from the tiny gap at the bottom of the door.

In that situation there were some believers who dwelt not only in these terrible earthly surroundings, but at the same time in heavenly places. Scarcely breathing, like asthmatics, they talked among themselves and with others about the sweet savour of sacrifices brought to God and of fragrances like those of heaven. They quoted scriptures about frankincense and myrrh, about roses and lilies.

The Jewish *Talmud* states that every meal at which the conversation is about something other than the Word of God is an idolatrous meal. When Christians were in the Rumanian prison of Piteshti, they tried to think about the Word of God while they ate, and to speak to each other about it. However, their torturers then decided to make them eat their own bodily waste. In Piteshti eating excrement and drinking urine was a daily routine. But while they did this, they thought of the Bible's words about the savour of God's good ointments. They meditated upon the perfumes described in the Word of God. So in prison one is made aware of how independent the spiritual life is from the life of the flesh.

A Russian priest, Nikiforov-Volghin, tells in his book *Dust on the Road* of the following story, told to him by a Christian he met in prison:

> One day I arrived home and heard somebody cry out. I found my wife, stabbed in the heart by somebody we knew. The murderer fell at my feet, begging my forgiveness. I said to him, 'Go, and do not do so anymore.' I went to the police and accepted responsibility for the crime. I was sentenced. Then in Krasnoyarsk prison one prisoner murdered another. For that, too, I accepted the blame. Now I am sentenced to life imprisonment. I could not do other than I did.
>
> Loving God, I look on all men as I look upon angels. My only prayer is, 'I am yours and you are mine – have mercy on me.' If you had not been a priest I would not have told you these things. You asked me why I am here, and you are entitled to the truth.

When this prisoner died it was as though heaven had opened. His last words were, 'Lord, I would like to continue to suffer for others; but thy will be done.' Those who are present at such a death, though prison squalor surrounds them, sometimes detect a heavenly fragrance. It is the odour of the high places in which the bride of Christ lives.

What is in his name?

In Shakespeare's *Romeo and Juliet*, the girl thought of her lover's name. The two belonged to warring families. He was a Montague, she a Capulet. Her family would never have consented to their marriage. So she advised him to change his name. 'What's in a name?' she asked. 'A rose by any other name would smell as sweet.' She was right about roses. A rose is called a 'rose' only in the English language; in other languages it has different names. And she was probably right about Romeo as well. She could have loved him even if his name had been Sebastian or Antonio.

I do not rule out the possibility that some love Jesus by another name. They have never heard the name 'Jesus' but they love Love. They love self-sacrifice, they love forgiveness and goodness. They love Divinity coming down to earth, and earthly beings uniting with Divinity. They love the poor and oppressed, those who represent Jesus on earth. You can love Jesus without knowing his name.

Many who call in prayer upon Krishna, Buddha or some other name may perhaps in reality mean 'Jesus'.

But with Jesus his name is important. In Hebrew it is *Yeshua*, which means 'salvation'. His very name proclaims what he stands for! You say 'Jesus', and it is like the pouring-out of ointment. Because of that name you know that there is salvation for you and for all people. Another of his names, 'Immanuel', means 'God is with us.'

Only the bride can say to the Saviour, 'Your name is an ointment poured forth.' Jesus did not have a good name in the world. He was called a glutton, a winebibber, a Samaritan (which at that time was the same as calling him a heretic); he was called a deceiver, they said that he had a devil, and so on. To this evil talk about Jesus the bride is deaf.

Souls who truly believe in Jesus are also widely slandered. In the Soviet press faithful pastors are called 'scoundrels, hooligans and villains'. They call Solzhenitsyn, the distinguished Nobel prizewinner, a traitor.

Concerning the finest Christians of all, the Communists spread the rumour that they are stool-pigeons of the communist authorities and secret agents of the police. As a result they are beaten up by their fellow-prisoners. However, they know that in the eyes of their Bridegroom, their name is good.

Holy love

The bride says, 'No wonder the virgins love you!' (1:3), and there is no jealousy in what she says. This is what distinguishes holy love from worldly love: not merely that we who love him are not jealous, but that we want many other souls to love him as well, and we desire him to pour out on them his caresses and his kisses.

In Australia a Christian lady stopped a young girl in the street. 'You look so sad! You are crying. I am a Christian. Could I be of help? Could I share your sorrow?'

'Thank you for your kindness,' replied the girl, 'but nobody can help me. The man I love has left me.'

Our sister said, 'Don't worry. I have a beautiful Bridegroom. I will give him to you.'

The girl, thinking she was being made fun of, said 'Why are you mocking my grief?'

Then our sister spoke to her about her heavenly Bridegroom – about Jesus. She explained that he can share his love with many, and yet to every one of them he gives all his love. The girl was brought to Christ.

Those who preach Jesus are not in competition with

one another. They are fellow-workers. So if a soul that was attached to one flock moves to join another, there is no need for sadness. It simply means that the spiritual atmosphere of the first flock did not suit that particular soul. No Christian teacher can claim that he is equally helpful to every individual.

It is not absolutely necessary that somebody should be a member of my church. Let him go to any church where he can grow spiritually, and I will accompany him there with my prayers.

'Draw me'

The bride says, 'Draw me, we will run after you. The king has brought me into his chambers; we will be glad and rejoice in you, we will remember your love more than wine; the upright love you' (1:4). She prays, 'Draw me.' She prays like this because she knows that she is still very far from him. 'Whilst we are at home in the body, we are absent from the Lord' (2 Corinthians 5:6). She prays like this because she longs to arrive at union with him.

It is not enough that he should draw her by convincing her. She does not have the moral power to follow her convictions. He must draw her with supernatural grace. He has to give her the will to come to him and the means to fulfil that will. He has said it himself: 'No man can come to me except the Father who has sent me draw him' (John 6:44). Nobody can come to Jesus by his own will.

Looking to the ascended Jesus, my prayer is 'Draw me.' What could hinder the fulfilment of this prayer? The way of ascension is open for everyone. Elijah was a man who had the same weaknesses as we all have, and he ascended into heaven. Everyone who consents to ride in a chariot of fire, as Elijah did, can ascend like him. Jesus said, 'He that shall humble himself shall be exalted' (Matthew 23:12).

We can come to where Jesus is; we can sit with him his throne (Revelation 3:21). But we have to follow the way he went, 'Who, being in the form of God . . . made himself of no reputation and took upon him the form of a servant and was made in the likeness of men; and being found in fashion as a man, he humbled himself and became obedient unto death, even the death of the Cross. Wherefore God has also highly exalted him and given him a name which is above every name.' (Philippians 2:6–9).

God is not only the Father of the Lord Jesus, but also our Father; and we can all ascend to him if we follow the way of Jesus. He lived for thirty-four years on earth in misery, poverty and unmeasured sorrows. Let us beware of wealth and exalted situations as of a burning fire, and our prayer to be drawn by him will be fulfilled.

Running after him

The bride says, 'Draw me, we will run after you.' We have not to walk after the Lord, but to run. The apostle Paul tells the believers, 'Let us *run* with patience' (Hebrews 12:1), 'So *run* that you may obtain the prize' (1 Corinthians 9:24); 'I therefore so *run*, not as uncertainly' (1 Corinthians 9:26). Only running can symbolise a living longing for God and a vigorous faith in him. Psalm 119:32 says, 'I will *run* the way of your commandments.'

It is written of the children of Israel that when they worshipped the golden calf, they 'sat down to eat and to drink' (Exodus 32:6). While Joseph was sitting, his brothers conferred as to how to sell him. (Genesis 37:25) It is a great catastrophe when the people of God sit down; they must run – run with all their heart, not listening to whispers or shouts from different sides, but violently rejecting any hindrance to their running. We have to run with our bodies stretched forward to seize the prize, before our feet arrive at our goal.

We have to run with extreme speed. Jesus told us we are lights. Light has greater speed than anything else in the natural world. In telling us that we are lights, Jesus told us to run with the speed of light. It is not the case that souls who run slower don't arrive in the end, but they do lose the prize reserved for those who arrive first.

In the bride's words, 'Draw *me*, *we* will run after *you*,' we observe the sudden passing from the singular to the plural in the midst of the sentence. The bride is saying, 'Jesus should draw *me* alone; then *we* – many of us – will run after him. You, Jesus, take care of me, drawing me with all your might, that I might influence others.' King David, too, says, 'Restore unto me the joy of your salvation, and uphold me with your free spirit, then I will teach transgressors your ways; and sinners shall be converted unto you.' (Psalm 51:12–13).

Let the words, 'We will run' stay in our minds. Are we believers who are running? This is easy to find out. The one who runs quickly covers a great distance in a short time. How great a distance have you covered since you came to God?

Communists who found Christ

Communists hate not only Christians, Jews, Moslems, patriots and those belonging to other political parties; they also hate one another. It once happened that five Russian Communists were in a prison cell, sentenced to death by their own comrades. While awaiting execution, one of them paced up and down in the cell, singing over and over, *Safe in the arms of Jesus*. Just those few words. The others asked him what he meant, but he did not know. He only knew that his mother had sung a song that began with those words. His mother died when he was young. What had remained fixed in his memory was that there is a place where one is safe. This place is called 'In the arms of Jesus.'

Another of the Communists said, 'I once saw an ikon of Jesus with his arms stretched out on a cross.' Now they knew two things – that Jesus died on a cross and that, in his arms, you are safe. A third said, 'In Russia, even now, we call the first day of the week *Voskresenie* (Resurrection). Is the one who was resurrected the same one who stretched out his arms on the cross? Is this what gives us safety, even in death?'

From these fragments of knowledge the Communists reconstructed the essence of the gospel. They went to their deaths singing, *Safe in the arms of Jesus*.

That is the speed at which the light was spread in death row. In no time at all, one had been drawn by Christ; and all the others followed him. You may not know very much about Jesus. But share quickly the little that you do know with others. There could be great consequences.

In Red China, where Christians were fiercely persecuted, somebody wrote on a wall, *God loves every man*. The next day he found more writing below: *even the Communists*. These words were probably written by a Red Guard who had found assurance that God loved him, too. The light had passed quickly from one soul to another.

The responsibility of soul-winners

The bride says, 'Draw me, we will run after you' (1:4). The faithful soul wins other people for Christ. By so doing, it takes upon itself a huge responsibility. In the Free World a soul-winner does not readily perceive this.

The man he wins for Christ will become a church member, sing in the choir, marry a nice Christian girl and lead a quiet Christian life. But to be a soul-winner in a Communist country – to be an evangelist in the Underground Church – burdens you with heavy problems.

When St Paul preached in Rome he knew that those who responded to his message could be thrown to the wild beasts and devoured in the circus arena. They could be crucified or burnt on stakes. Should he preach, in such circumstances? Or would it be better for him to remain silent? Is it right to propagate an idea if it will bring men to prison, to torture and to death? How many unbelieving wives, parents and children must have cursed Paul, because his preaching brought such sorrow to their families? But when you are drawn by Jesus, you must make others run after him.

I was in jail with a man whom Traian Dorz, the famous Rumanian poet, had brought to Christ. He was sentenced for his faith, and he had left a wife and six children at home. I asked him, 'Are you resentful towards Dorz, for taking you out of your life of tranquillity and setting you upon this dangerous path?' He said, 'I can't thank him enough.'

During World War II, Mrs Roosevelt, the wife of the President of the USA, carried in her purse this prayer:

> *Dear Lord,*
> *Lest I continue*
> *My complacent way,*
> *Help me to remember*
> *Somewhere out there*
> *A man died for me today.*
> *As long as this fight continues,*
> *I then must ask and answer –*
> *Am I worth dying for?*

Every ruler and every officer who sends soldiers to die – yes, every conscientious citizen – must ask himself or herself the same question.

In the Underground Church the pastor gives assignments to his church members which might result in their death. He asks them to organize secret printing presses, to secretly transport Christian literature from place to place. If they are caught these people will go to prison. Because of those printing presses, many people have died.

The Christian Mission to the Communist World has sent couriers into Communist countries to smuggle holy books in. One of these, Wang-Shin-Mei, was beaten to death in China. Two others, Tom White and Mel Bailey, were caught in Cuba; they received prison sentences of twenty-three years each. Others were wounded while taking Bibles into Communist Mozambique.

A soul-winner in the Underground Church is not allowed to be complacent. He must remember that his brothers and sisters may die for what he has told them to believe and to do.

In the Free World, Christians must be taught to carry crosses and to learn to renounce. The soul-winner must know and practise this himself, before he teaches it to others.

In the king's chambers

The bride prayed, 'Draw me', and the prayer was granted immediately. The king brought her into his chambers.

We read of Blessed Ann Marie Taigi (1769–1837), a woman of simple background and mother of seven children, that she saw a mysterious sun suspended before her, a little above head height. By its light she saw all the visible and invisible things of earth. She penetrated also into the depths of the abyss and into the high places of heaven, just as St Paul rose to the third heaven (2 Corinthians 12:2). With great clarity she observed the fates of diverse men and the secrets of nature and grace. She could discern the secret thoughts of people near at hand and far away.

For her, there was no time; she could see men and events in the past and the future. Everything happened in that single moment, in the mystical sun. In one glance she perceived a multitude of things, with perfect knowledge and in complete detail.

Ignatius of Loyola saw, in a rapture, divine things. While sitting near a river and allowing his eyes to rest on the water, his sight was opened and he understood many things – secrets of faith and revelations from the realm of natural science – with such an overwhelming clarity that he had no doubt it was a revelation from God.

These were people who had been in the King's chambers. I have myself known men who have been there. In jail, I was thrown together with a Christian sentenced to death. He sang songs which he had composed. He told us, 'Death does not scare me. I sing here; I will do the same after I am shot. Only the songs will be different. Here, my hymns somehow centre around myself, telling of my longings, how sinful I have been, how I was saved, although the Lord taught us in his prayer to pray without using the word "I". Heavenly songs are different. The angels sing that God is thrice holy, and that the earth is filled with his glory. They rejoice over it, and they have nothing to ask. About themselves they say nothing, neither good nor bad. At Christ's birth they sang "Glory to God in the highest, and on earth, peace to men on whom his favour rests." There was no petition for personal needs.'

My Christian cellmate went to his execution singing one of the new songs which he had learned in the chambers of Jesus. In his spirit, he had been in heavenly Jerusalem, the city far away, before his physical death. We are all meant to visit the chambers of Jesus and to learn these new songs.

'We will be glad'

The bride says, 'The king has brought me into his chambers: we will be glad and rejoice in you' (1:4). The grace given her affects many others. Once again she passes from the singular case to the plural: 'The king has brought *me* into his chambers; *we* will rejoice.' It is enough that one single soul should be in right fellowship with God, and the whole Church of which he is a part will be blessed, and will have joy and gladness.

There are no useless words in the Bible. It is written, 'We will be glad and rejoice,' and it might seem that this is repetitious. But there is a progression here from inner joy to outward gladness. Gladness can be faked. It must be united to a joy in the heart which makes it genuine.

Many people display gladness even though their stony hearts have been long incapable of knowing true joy. God continually insists that joy and gladness must go together; there should be neither laughter without the heart's participation, nor a joy in the heart too miserly to show itself outwardly and thus gladden others. The archangel Gabriel said to Zacharias the priest, 'You shall have joy and gladness' (Luke 1:14). The prodigal son's father said to his other son, 'It was meet that we should make merry, and be glad: for this your brother was dead, and is alive again' (Luke 15:32). Jesus tells us to 'rejoice . . . and leap for joy' (Luke 6:23). So rejoicing should be accompanied by outward signs of jubilation.

Loving unto death

The bride says, 'We will remember your love more than wine' (1:4). The wine represents the king's gifts, as distinguished from his person. That he himself unites with us is of more value to humanity than all the things he gives to us.

'The upright [literally, 'uprighteousnesses'] love you.' They love Jesus even unto death. Bishop Seraphim of Phanarion in Greece was martyred, on 4 December 1601. He had been falsely accused of plotting and rebelling against the Turks. They shouted at him, 'Rebel and subverter of our authority! Behold, thou hast come into our hands, and thou wilt receive that which is thy due – unless, perchance, thou shouldst wish to abandon thy faith and become a Moslem. Then we would forgive thee, and honour thee greatly, for by this we would know that thou hadst repented and become as one with us.'

The saint was an upright man who loved Jesus. He desired martyrdom for Christ and did not become in the least fainthearted. He said to them with a clear and serene countenance, 'I will never agree in any circumstances to forsake my faith, so that I might be spared my death. I will never forsake my most sweet Jesus, my God and my Creator.

'Now, because I suffer unjustly, I have the more hope on that account that I shall receive from my Master even greater honour. I would never deny my faith; nor shall I ever be separated from my sweetest Master and God, Jesus Christ. Though I shall die ten thousand deaths for his holy name, I would count it all joy and gladness. O, Ruler! Be it slaughter or mutilation, do whatsoever is within thy power.'

The ruler, Hamouza Bey, then ordered him to be flogged and his nose to be cut into small pieces. This upright man loved Jesus. He endured all these torments as if they were happening to somebody else, thanking God and blessing him.

The next morning he appeared before Hamouza Bey again, and his attitude was the same. 'I will never abandon my Lord Jesus, my Creator who shaped me, only to believe in a mortal man – an illiterate – an enemy and blasphemer of my Christ!'

They tore him to pieces. But even his merciless executioners marvelled to see that he endured it all with thanksgiving, and that his face was bright and joyous as if he were at a feast. In the end he was impaled.

Legends often arise around such great saints. It is said that his head and those of others condemned as criminals were placed on spears and arranged in a row facing west. This was done each evening, and by morning the heads would be as they had left them, except for that of Seraphim: his head would be found looking toward the east, towards Jerusalem, the Holy City.

The Kenyan periodical *Target* reported that the Anglican Bishop of Uganda, Janani Luwum, was shot in front of President Amin because he refused to kneel and beg for mercy. The same demonic spirit seems to be at work in Communist Cuba as well. Fidel Castro attended the execution by firing squad of a Christian. As his hands were tied behind his back, Castro urged him, 'Kneel, and beg for your life.' The Christian shouted back 'I kneel for no man!' A sharp-shooter put a bullet first through one knee, then the other. Castro exulted: 'See! We have made you kneel!' The man was finished off slowly by being shot through the non-vital parts of the body, so that the agony was prolonged. This incident is described by John Martino in his book *I was Castro's prisoner*.

The devil himself works through these anti-Christian dictators. We are reminded of the words he addressed to the Lord: 'All these things will I give you, if you will fall down and worship me' (Matthew 4:9).

Christians such as these I have described are each one a

personification of 'uprighteousness.' Therefore the Hebrew text says, 'Uprighteousnesses love you.'

'Black and comely'

The bride says, 'I am black [but] comely, O you daughters of Jerusalem,' (1:5). An important emendation to the translation is needed here in the Authorized Version. We read, 'I am black but comely.' This gives the impression that black people are usually ugly, and that Solomon's bride was an exception, comely despite her blackness. There is no trace of this idea in the Hebrew original, which reads simply, 'I am black *and* comely.' There are as many beautiful black girls as beautiful white girls or yellow girls. There is no hint of racism in this verse.

Blackness is absence of light, and it is in this sense that the Bible uses the term. The Church is black because some believers do not obey God; but she is beautiful because of her saints and perfect Christians. She is black in the eyes of men, because those whose souls are blind cannot perceive the beauty of the kingdom of God within us, but she is beautiful before God.

We are black because of our own weakness, but beautiful and strong through God's grace, which is ours in abundance. A man can be black because he is guilty of many sins, but beautiful in God's eyes from the very moment he puts his joyful trust in Jesus, the Saviour of sinners, who forgives him and will change his soul.

Today's decayed Church can be black on account of her deeds, but she is beautiful on account of those who have gone before in faith. She is beloved because of the first generation of Christians who were aflame with gentle love, just as Israel, even though it rejected Jesus, remains beloved because of the Jewish patriarchs. Though she may be blackened by persecution, the Church is beautiful through her penitence. She may be weak, but the words of Psalm 45 apply to her: 'The king's daughter is all glorious within' (verse 13).

Never be afraid when you discover your weakness and sinfulness, when you discover the lack of light or blackness. You are only one in a large flock. A small part of a body can be affected by disease while the body as a whole remains healthy. Similarly you are 'healthy' or beautiful by virtue of the Church to which you belong, which possesses the beautiful characters of the saints. Their beauty reflects upon you.

In Red China, a wedding took place at an execution ground. Zhou Wen Yong and Chen Tie-Zhun had been workers together in the Underground Church and had both been sentenced to death. They were in love. At the place of execution Zhou asked Chen, 'Will you be my wife?' She consented. He declared 'So we are married before God! Let the Communist bullet be the seal of our wedding. We will feast our marriage in paradise.'

A Soviet prisoner wrote from jail, 'I bow my head in humility before our mother, the Church. I thank God for the education she gave me. The Church of Christ has many sufferings, but also an overflow of joy. In the Siberian cold, we warmed the icy winter's embraces with the Word of God.'

Let us thank God that we belong to this Church which has such saints as members, even if we ourselves are unworthy. We are black and beautiful.

Every believer is tempted at some time to think, 'You, who are so black – how can you speak about the Lord?' Every preacher at some time thinks, 'How can I, who am so wicked, even climb into the pulpit?' Our courage evaporates when we consider what state we are in.

But look at the apostle Peter. He, who had denied Christ with oaths and curses, stood in the Jerusalem marketplace and rebuked the people: '*You* denied the Holy One and the Just' (Acts 3:14). He who had himself committed this very sin, in the most heinous manner, rebuked others for the same sin, though they were much less guilty. He could do this because he knew that he was not only black but beautiful – not only sinful, but also forgiven and beloved by God. The darkness in him did not make Peter despair. He knew he was wicked, but he also knew that when he preached, it was not him speaking but Christ, who lived in him.

The night is black, but it gives rest to the earth. Black bread is very nutritious. A pastor who by his own deeds is in darkness but is beautiful by the grace he receives from God, can feed a hungry flock. I trust Jesus' taste more than my own! I see myself as black, he sees me as beautiful. He sees himself mirrored in us. He sees us as we shall be.

The bride compares her blackness to that of the tents of Kedar and the curtains of Solomon (1:5). Kedar was a district of Arabia inhabited by Bedouins. They made their tents from black goat hair. The curtains at Solomon's palace were also said to be black. Black curtains keep out the light from a room. This image means that great care was necessary to ensure that the many sins committed by the bride should not come to light.

Do not be critical

The bride admonishes, 'Look not upon me as being blackish' [the meaning of the Hebrew word] 'because the sun has looked upon me' (1:6). She had described herself as 'black' (shechorah), but now, pondering the fact that she is also beautiful, she no longer calls herself 'black'. She is only 'blackish' (shecharchoret). Men should not even regard her as that. They should learn to see her beautiful side.

The believer should regard nobody as 'black'; he should be careful not to slander even his weakest brother. The apostle Peter says, 'God has shown me that I should not call any man common or unclean' (Acts 10:28). The bride is blackish, but listen to her defence! 'I am blackish because the sun has looked upon me. My mother's children were angry with me; they made me the keeper of the vineyards.' If my brother has sinned, the reason may be the many sufferings, temptations and persecutions which he has endured. When the Spirit of God does his work, my brother will confess his sins himself, like the bride in Solomon's Song.

To explain how she came to be 'blackish', she reviews her past life. 'My mother's children' – that is, the members of the Church, which is the believer's mother – 'were angry with me; they made me the keeper of the vineyards' – an occupation in which you get heavily sunburnt. 'I have been given great assignments,' the bride complains. 'I have been appointed a pastor, a teacher of the brethren.' Other believers might well envy her situation, but it was in that situation that she was burned by the sun and became blackish.

Christians, don't compete for the honour of being leaders in the Church. It is a calling that should make you tremble. Saint James writes, 'My brethren, be not many masters, knowing that we shall receive the greater condemnation' (3:1). Christians, don't judge. Coventry Cathedral in England was destroyed by German bombs during World War II. When it was rebuilt two charred logs from the old building were made into a cross bearing the inscription, 'Father, forgive'. There was no 'them' at the end. The British knew that they too needed to be forgiven.

Terrorists sin. So do all Arabs who do not love Zionists.

And Zionists have committed sins towards Arabs. Communists sin. Christians in Communist countries sin too, because they are not being holy and zealous enough to prevent men from becoming Communists. The best of pastors sin more than all of these. God gives them a vision, but they neglect many of their duties.

For all of us, our only hope is the Lord's sacrifice on Good Friday; the Easter event, his resurrection, is our only source of peace. So do not misuse your mouth by criticizing, and especially by criticizing the bride of Christ.

The dangers of the pastorate

Be very cautious before you accept the office of pastor, a keeper in God's vineyard. The believer's preference is for a hidden life with God. Listen to a biblical parable:

> Once, the trees went forth to anoint a king over them. And they said to the olive tree, 'Reign over us.' But the olive tree said unto them, 'Should I leave my fatness wherewith by me they honour God and man, and go to be promoted over the trees?'
>
> And the trees said to the fig tree, 'You come and reign over us.' But the fig tree said unto them, 'Should I forsake my sweetness, and my good fruit, and go to be promoted over the trees?'
>
> Then said the trees unto the vine, 'You come and reign over us.' And the vine said to them, 'Should I leave my wine, which cheers God and man, and go to be promoted over the trees?'
>
> Then said all the trees unto the bramble, 'You come and reign over us.'
>
> And the bramble said unto the trees, 'If in truth you

anoint me king over you, then come and put your trust in my shadow. And if not, let fire come out of the thistle and devour the cedars of Lebanon (Judges 9:8–17).

Only valueless Christians long for important positions in the Church of God and rejoice when they are given them. They are misguided, because important positions in the Church leave no time for maintaining the beauty of your own vineyard. You become so concerned with caring for others that you don't care about yourself. You will be in danger of the same catastrophe which overcame ancient Israel, to whom the apostle Paul wrote: 'You therefore who teach another, do you not teach yourself? You who preach that a man should not steal, do you steal? You who say that a man should not commit adultery, do you commit adultery? You who abhor idols, do you commit sacrilege?' (Romans 2:21–22).

The only man who should become a pastor or a missionary is the man who cannot be anything else. He who can say with the prophet Jeremiah, 'His word was in my heart as a burning fire shut up in my bones, and I was weary with forebearing, and I could not stay' (Jeremiah 20:9). Young converts, don't push yourselves forward for leading positions in the churches and in missions! Don't begin preaching at the earliest opportunity out of a sense of obligation! It is better to keep the beauty of your own vineyard.

Where can he be found?

The bride says, 'Tell me, O you whom my soul loves, where you feed, where you make your flock to rest at noon: for why should I be as one that turns aside by the flocks of your companions?' (1:7). She gives Jesus a beautiful name, 'You Whom My Soul Loves'. The Church is the beloved of God's soul, and God is the Beloved of our souls.

The bride wants to know the exact place where her Beloved is. She wants to go to the place where he rests, where he feeds his flock, because in her diffidence she does not want to distract him from his preoccupations by asking him to come to her. She will go to him, and will be able to speak with him while helping him in his work. She will not abuse his time. But she must know exactly where he is. She does not want to wander around among his companions' flocks. She does not want to find herself among the flocks of the other founders of religions, who are not like him.

Jesus has given us an exact address where we can find him. It is written that on the day of the Last Judgement, men will hear these words from him: 'I was in prison and you came to me,' or these: 'I was in prison, and you visited me not' (Matthew 25:36, 43). And then he will explain: 'Verily I say unto you, inasmuch as you have done it . . . [or] did it not to one of the least of these my brethren, you have done it . . . [or] did it not unto me' (25:40, 45). Whoever wishes to meet Jesus must meet him in places where brothers and sisters of Jesus are hungry, thirsty, naked, unwanted, sick or in prison. Whoever keeps himself distant from these places remains distant from Jesus.

In his book *The Unmasking*, G. Dumitrescu – a former jail inmate in Communist Rumania – writes:

Prisoners were so tortured that nobody dared to use a hand for making the sign of the Cross. We did it with our tongues. We had to stay the whole day with hands lifted, even when at toilet. We had to put the dish with food on the floor, kneel near it, and lick the food without using the hands. We were animals. The food burned our lips. We were beaten with sticks on the shinbones, but could not rub our feet. The hands had to stay unmoved. Every prisoner was asked to beat his best friend, his brother in faith. If he refused, the brethren were tortured until they agreed to beat him with truncheons on the soles.

The prisoner, Nuti Patrashcanu, had become a sadistic torturer of his friends. Then they tortured him almost to death. Twelve of them sat on his body; he excreted and was made to eat his own excrement.

The Patrashcanu mentioned above later shared a prison cell with me, and God gave me the grace to bring him to Christ. His bride, who was free, was also converted. He later died in jail.

The last words of the Christian Sherban Gheorge, who was killed in an atrocious manner in Piteshti, still echo in our ears: 'The Communists' crimes are too horrible. I can't pray for them to God from a distance. I must go to him to speak on their behalf. Do not avenge my death.'

Jesus' companions

The bride says, 'Why should I be as one that turns aside by the flocks of your companions?' (1:7). In this verse the founders of other religions are called the companions of Jesus, not his competitors. Jesus has no competition. He is not threatened by all those who have inscribed high thoughts about God in the Vedas of the Indians and in the holy books of other nations; he is not threatened by Confucius, Lao-Tzu, Buddha, Muhammed and other founders of religion who, in the measure of the light which they had, tried to bring men to better ways.

The bride's question as to where the Beloved sleeps arises from a legitimate desire to see his face; but it does not receive a direct answer. On the last evening, Thomas asked the Lord, 'We know not where you are going: and how can we know the way?' (John 14:5). But Jesus had already replied: 'Where I go you know, and the way you know' (14:4). He concedes to no man the possibility that he would not know what his duty is, that somebody sincerely seeking the King of Kings would not be able to distinguish between him and one of his companions or a deceiver, that he would not know how to distinguish betwen the lilies with which he feeds his flock and the simple grass of the others. That would be to despair of human thought. Jesus believes that men are capable of thinking correctly.

Only love Jesus with a perfect love, from your whole heart, and you will know where he feeds his flock as surely as every man who loves drugs or alcohol knows where to find them. 'What man is he that fears the Lord? Him shall he teach in the way that he shall choose' (Psalm 25:12). The difficulty is not lack of knowledge, but a moral weakness. His bride cannot make the decision to go to the place of deep suffering, which is the surest place of encounter with the greatly-Beloved.

Would you like to know where Jesus feeds his flock? Deny yourself and take up your cross. Then you can be sure of following him. Would you like to know where he rests at noon? Once, he rested in the bosom of the Father; now he rests in the heart of every believer who gives him room. But he is pre-eminently resting in the hearts of the believers who are undergoing suffering; in the hearts of those who have purified themselves from attachment to created things, so that they may remain entirely indwelling in the Creator.

I remember a Good Friday in a cell in the Rumanian jail, Jilava. We were all very hungry, but that day when the bowl of gruel was brought we refused to eat. We fasted. Good Friday is the only fast-day described by the Lord himself: 'The days will come, when the bridegroom shall be taken from them, and then they shall fast' (Matthew 9:15). Days of fasting, with deep repentance for our past sins, are the greatest gifts anybody can give to the Underground Church and the missions which help it.

As a punishment for refusing the food on Good Friday we were made to stand to attention for the whole of Easter morning. That provided a captive audience for a sermon! If anybody had desired to be with Jesus on that day, he should have travelled in spirit to be in fellowship with us. Jesus was in jail with his disciples on that day. Prison is one of the places where we should look for him. I wonder at the numbers of Christians from the Free World who visit Communist countries but never ask permission to visit a jail and encourage their brothers and sisters in pain.

In Solomon's Song Jesus did not say directly where he feeds his flock. He wants us to think for ourselves. But on the Day of Judgement we will be reproached or approved, according to whether or not we have been among this world's sufferers.

By the footsteps of the flock

In the Song, Jesus' reply to the bride's question is: 'If you do not know yourself' – so the Hebrew reads – 'O you fairest among women, go your way forth by the footsteps of the flock, and feed your kids by the shepherds' tents' (1:8). The Bridegroom calls her, 'The fairest among women.' Nothing is more beautiful in God's sight than a believing soul. He is blind to its weaknesses.

The Bridegroom shows us a simple way to find him. If she wishes with all her heart to come to where he is, the bride must 'go by the footsteps of the flock.' In this world there are men who bear the visible sign of being Jesus' sheep. Go after them; imitate their example. Do as they do. They are in fellowship with Jesus. If you follow in their footsteps you will come into fellowship with him too.

When in Central Africa the first pygmy came to believe in Jesus, another pygmy, Kiwebulaya, who could not understand what his friend was talking about, decided to follow him to find out the secret of his changed life. One day he saw him leave the village. He went after him, unobserved, into the jungle. He watched his friend kneel in the grass, fold his hands, and speak with his new invisible friend Jesus.

Now Kiwebulaya knew what he had to do. After his friend had finished praying and departed, he went to the same place, knelt in the depressions in the grass left by his friend, folded his hands as he had done and said, 'Jesus, you who made my friend happy, make me happy too.'

A voice replied: 'Come unto me, you pygmy who labour and are heavy laden, and I will give you rest.' Kiwebulaya said, 'I would come to you, Jesus, but I don't know how.' He received a reply again: 'I will be with you always.' When he rose from his praying, Kiwebulaya's face shone with happiness just as his friend's face shone. He had come to where Jesus was by following in the footsteps of one of his sheep.

But be very careful that those whom you follow are really Jesus' sheep. To use another animal analogy, hunters sometimes have useless dogs. They run after the real hunting dogs, and if they were persistent they would arrive at the kill with the others. But instead they stop at every bush and every curiosity. The hunting dogs we should follow are the real ones, which go through fire and water.

The Bible says, 'Walk in the way of good men, and keep the paths of the righteous' (Proverbs 2:20). Paul says, 'Be followers of me, even as I also am of Christ' (1 Corinthians 11:1). He also says, 'Be not slothful, but followers of them who through faith and patience inherit the promises' (Hebrews 6:12). The best way of advancing in the life of faith is to take as our examples the most worthy believers of the Church's history, not those who have the latest fanciful doctrines. In art galleries one can see many young painters copying the masterpieces of painters of the past. Young believers must copy the outstanding saints of the past.

When the Communists took over Angola, they began to threaten and persecute the Christians. Those who were true believers remained unafraid. One Sunday morning the Communist soldiers entered the Evangelical Church in the town of Chiasso. They drove cattle into the church, slaughtered them and mounted the animals' heads on the pulpit and the communion table. A sign on the pulpit announced, 'These are the gods you now worship.'

The believers were given a choice: either to die, or to deny their faith. The pastor, Aurelio Chicanha, and 150 church members remained steadfast and were murdered there and then. The mission compound was turned into a military base. Similar killings and appropriations of churches have happened in Chissamba, Dondi, Bungue and Elemde.

These believers were real sheep, whose example we can follow. Not all of us are called to die a martyr's death, but all of us are called to have the same spirit of self-sacrifice and love to the very end as these martyrs had.

My former fellow-prisoner Ion Stanescu, a Rumanian Orthodox deacon, died from tortures suffered in prison. He once told me the following story.

Colonel Albon, the director of the slave labour camp where Stanescu was imprisoned, was informed that someone had dared to preach in Stanescu's cell. He entered carrying a cane and demanded to know the culprit. When nobody answered, he said, 'Well then, everybody will be flogged. Unbutton!'

He started at one end of the cell, and there was the usual yelling and tears. When he came to Stanescu, he said, 'Not ready yet? Strip this minute!' Stanescu replied, 'Neither I nor the others will be beaten any more. There is a God in heaven, and he will judge you.'

With that the fate of Stanescu appeared to be sealed. Surely he would be beaten to death! But just at that moment, a guard entered the cell and said, 'Colonel, you are wanted urgently in the office. Some generals have come from the Ministry.' Albon left, saying to Stanescu, 'We will see each other again soon.'

However, the generals arrested the colonel (Communists hate and jail one another for no apparent reason) and, after an hour, Albon was back in the cell, this time as a prisoner. Many of the inmates jumped to lynch him. But Stanescu defended his defeated enemy with his own body, taking many blows himself as he protected the torturer from the beaten prisoners.

Stanescu was a real priest. We have to follow in the footsteps of men like this, loving our enemies but also resisting their evil deeds.

It is easy to walk 'by the footsteps of the flock' because sheep follow only beaten tracks, and will never take even one step to the right or to the left away from it. But again, let us be careful to walk only by the path of Jesus' sheep. Not all sheep have virtues to be imitated. Some can be very cruel. Any farmer will tell you about sheep who, by withholding milk, let their lambs die of starvation. Sometimes they even smash the lambs' heads against a wall. Also, certain sheep of different breeds hate one another; those of the Hampshire breed cannot tolerate those of the Suffolk breed. Avoid Christian sheep of this kind.

Where to feed our kids

The Bridegroom tells the bride, 'Feed your kids beside the

shepherds' tents.' The meaning of these words is clarified by this Jewish proverb: 'If you wish to smell pleasant, stand near those who sell perfumes.' The nearer a faithful soul is to his pastor, the more he will make his valuable teachings his own and the clearer he will see the face of Jesus.

Saint Basil the Great said, 'When you are sick, you don't go to any physician but the best. Neither should you listen to sermons at random. Seek the pastor who prepares conscientiously the best food for your souls.' The leaders of the Church must take care that only men of spiritual maturity and great abilities preach. These words of the Bridegroom are also a challenge to pastors. The believer will have to feed his kids beside the shepherds' tents. Can somebody feed the kids near you? Are you like Jesus, a good man on the bosom of whom others are able to rest?

We can take as an example Gheorge Calciu, the Rumanian Underground priest. He is Orthodox, but had warm brotherly relations with the persecuted Protestants. He was at one time a fellow-prisoner of mine. Arrested at the age of twenty-one, he spent twenty-two years in jail for belonging to a patriotic organisation. In jail he suffered the worst torture. He was one of those forced to eat his own excrement and to drink his own urine. One could escape these atrocities by claiming to have been re-educated in the Communist spirit and proving it by torturing one's friends. Calciu cracked for a while under the pressure, but he received grace from God and he was converted. Freed, he became an Orthodox priest and a heroic one. All fear to which he had yielded for a while was gone. From great depths of sin he rebounded to the heights of holiness. Seminary students and other young people flocked to hear him preach. When the Communists locked the door of the seminary to prevent students from going to hear him, the students jumped in through the windows. The Communists locked the church; Calciu preached on its steps. He protested about the tearing-down of Orthodox churches in Bucharest and in the provincial towns, though he was warned that in Communist countries priests must be on the side of the atheists who are in power.

He continued his stand despite threats of detention in a lunatic asylum. Later he was sentenced to ten years in prison. Calciu valued courage, the rare gift of God, like a precious stone. From his story we can see that a man who has sinned can become a good pastor, near whose tents brides of Christ can feed their kids.

Pharaoh's chariots

The Bridegroom says to the bride, 'I have compared you, O my love, to a company of horses in Pharaoh's chariots.' With these words he rebukes the numerous believers who ignore the advice that they should follow in the footsteps of the flock. On first reading the comparison is hard to understand. How could he compare his beloved, 'the most beautiful among women', to horses?

Solomon's Song is an ancient book, written in a time when people thought about animals differently to us today. Julius Caesar erected a marble effigy of his horse in a temple. The Emperor Nero nominated his horse to be a senator. The Emperor Caligula made his horse a consul and invited the animal to dinner and waited upon him.

In the Bible we find these words 'The Lord of Hosts has visited his flock, the house of Judah, and has made them as his goodly horse in the battle' (Zechariah 10:3). The patriarch Jacob pays his son a compliment by saying, 'Issachar is a strong ass' (Genesis 49:14). Jesus calls his believers 'sheep'.

There is nothing insulting in comparing a human being

to an animal. Ancient Egypt was famous for its horses, which were the finest in the world, so the Bridegroom compared his beloved girl to a horse. But these words also contain a rebuke. Huge possibilities of spiritual victories lie ahead. He wishes to lead us in *his* chariot of trials. Seated there, we can conquer all fears, temptations and sins. But instead of accepting his invitation, we allow ourselves to be harnessed to the chariot of Pharaoh. We do not sit with him *in* the chariot. We have to pull it, and in it Pharaoh sits alone.

Why should we sweat in his service? Why should we draw his cart? Why should we be harnessed to the chariot of sin? Why be yoked in an uncomfortable yoke with unbelievers? Why does a believing soul need to stoop to dirty politics – even dirty ecclesiastical politics? You might only be a horse pulling the chariot of some unbelieving president or prime minister who cares nothing for you. What good are dishonest transactions and ugly amusements to you? Don't let yourself be harnessed to Pharaoh's chariot. Ride with the noblemen in Jesus' chariot of triumph.

Being harnessed to Pharaoh's chariot is not pleasant. Drawings from ancient bas-reliefs in the Nile region show that the ancient Egyptians did not understand the anatomy of the horse, nor the correct way to harness it. They attached the reins to the horse's throat, almost suffocating it. Instead of allowing its neck to be extended in the normal way, they held the head in line with its chest, sometimes pulled even back further. Just as the ancient Egyptians did not know the horse's anatomy, neither do Pharaohs know the intimate structure of a believer's soul. They harness these souls in a way that torments them.

It is sad that the Bridegroom must so rebuke his bride. There are Christians who support the terrorist Palestine Liberation Organisation. There are Jewish Christians in Israel supporting the anti-Arab measures of their government. There are Christians who support the Communist guerrilla movements in the Third World. Other Christians defend the Soviet persecutors of the Church or other dictatorships. Many believers are involved in unjust transactions, and extramarital relationships and in the world of amusement are in places where they should not be. It is sad that brides of Christ should be harnessed to Pharaoh's chariots!

How to rebuke

But even as he rebukes, the Bridegroom uses words of gentleness. He says, 'I compare you, *O my love*, to a company of horses in Pharaoh's chariots.' She who causes him sadness is addressed, 'O my love'. Let us also learn to sweeten our reproofs with good words. Praise must go hand in hand with rebuke.

In his Epistles St Paul sometimes rebukes believers with great harshness, but his rebukes were accepted because they never arrived unaccompanied. They came with gentle words, expressing appreciation of the good qualities in the believers. Before rebuking them, he writes to the Romans, 'First, I thank my God through Jesus Christ for you all, that your faith is spoken of throughout the whole world' (Romans 1:8); to the Philippians; 'I thank my God upon every remembrance of you' (Philippians 1:3); to the Thessalonians, 'We give thanks to God always for you all, making mention of you in our prayers' (1 Thessalonians 1:2). This is how one removes the bitterness of rebuke.

Antonina was the abbess of the women's convent in the town of Kizliar in the Soviet Caucasus. In the early days of the Revolution, when the plundering of monasteries was a common occurrence, a mob of Bolshevik bandits broke into the convent. They looted and destroyed, and shot dead several nuns who resisted them. The abbess Antonina fled to the convent of Vladikavkas; but posters were displayed locally offering a reward of 3,000 roubles to anybody reporting the whereabouts of the former abbess of Kizliar. The Communists could not trace her, though they suspected that she was concealed in another convent.

Time passed. Then a young girl arrived at the convent. With many tears she begged the abbess of Vladikavkas to take her in, saying that her father and mother had been killed and their estate burgled. She played the part so well that she succeeded in winning the confidence of the abbess who, out of sympathy, not only took the girl in and was kind to her but soon even confided to her the secret that Antonina was in hiding there.

Soon after this the girl disappeared. She had been an agent of the secret police, looking for Antonina. That night the militia surrounded the convent. Nobody could escape. They broke in to search, demanding that the abbess should be given up. When the two cell attendants went upstairs to tell Antonina what was happening, she said, 'Well, what can I do? If it pleases the Lord that they find me, let it be so. But if it is not his will, he will close people's eyes; they, seeing me, will not see me. Come, we will go out in front of them.'

The nuns put a sheepskin coat on her, and the three women went down the stairs and simply walked out of the convent gate, before the very eyes of all the Red Army soldiers. They had not gone far when they heard the commander shouting. 'Who just went out of the gate? Who was let out?'

'We saw nobody,' answered the soldiers.

'What do you mean?' retorted the angry commander. 'Someone just left in a white sheepskin coat, accompanied by two nuns.'

Before her martyr death several years later, Antonina

met the girl who had informed on her. She did not start with words of rebuke, but said to her, 'I valued very much the tears you shed when asking to be received as a nun in the convent. It is very difficult to fake tears. They must have come from a heart in whose depths there is a spark of genuine love for Christ. You have been misused. You were young, you did not know what you were doing. But God did not only see you denounce me. He heard those prayers which you said, in which not all was falsehood. There may have been an occasional note of sincerity. God will pity your soul; only repent.' There was so much friendliness, spiritual beauty and complete lack of resentment in the words of Abbess Antonina that the girl's heart was pierced. She became a real believer in Christ. Let us also learn to rebuke like this.

Holy nonsense

The Bridegroom says, 'Your cheeks are comely with rows of jewels, your neck with chains of gold' (1:10). The words 'of jewels' and 'of gold' have been added by the translators to make sense of the Hebrew text. They are not in the original. The authors of the *Septuagint*, who were the first to translate the Old Testament into Greek, also tried to make sense of the text and wrote, 'How beautiful are your cheeks as the turtledove's.' But doves have no cheeks! The *Targum* – the Aramaic translation – renders it, 'Your cheeks are comely with bridles.' What does all this mean?

We are prejudiced. We think that everything in the Bible must make sense. If we don't find a meaning we invent one. But not all the Bible consists of logical, reasonable, purposeful thoughts. Much of it is the expression of a wide gamut of feelings, of reactions to events, or of impulse. Not all the Bible makes sense, and life and the human mind have their nonsensical features also. Nobody who fails to give nonsense a place can mirror the whole of reality in his religious writings. Depths of emotion cause lovers to talk a great deal of nonsense. How much of it there is in the conversation of Romeo and Juliet!

The simplest explanation is that Solomon wished to compliment his bride; saying, 'Your cheeks are comely.' They were so comely that instead of comparing them to something he just kissed them. But then he wanted to convey something more. He used the word *batorim*, which can mean 'turtledoves' or possibly 'bridles'. And then, instead of explaining himself further, he bestowed further kisses.

Then he said, 'Your neck is chains.' What would he have added? 'Of gold'? Or did he, perhaps, imagine his bride with iron chains on her neck, bound to the poles or stakes on which she was to be sacrificed by her captors? Or did he see her chained like those unfortunate women who were driven from Africa to America in slavery, with iron chains round their necks? In any event, he did not continue. Her neck was too comely for him to think of it being so abused. He preferred to kiss it.

No life is complete without its nonsensical side. Let us sanctify it.

God's jewels

The Bridegroom promises the bride, 'We will make you borders of gold with studs of silver' (1:11). God is a lover of beauty. He made his heavenly city of pure gold; its gates of pearls; its foundations of costly stones. The places where believers gathered for worship were to be beautiful also, the religious services solemn. The individual believer's soul must also have beauty, and this we can obtain through faith. The human soul cannot ornament herself. God is the one who ornaments and perfects her. God the Father, God the Son and God the Holy Spirit work at this; therefore the plural is used here: '*We* will make . . .'

God's jewels are unusual. Golden objects are normally given studs of costly stones or platinum, which increase their value. God gives them studs of silver, which decrease it. He gives us spiritual truth – which is gold – in the shape of simple human words, because otherwise we could not wear it. He made the Eternal Word, his Son, to have the body of an obedient servant, so that he could live among us. He puts studs of the silver of humility in the golden chains of the truth.

It is not always the most celebrated Christians – those who have studs of diamonds in their chains of gold – who are the best Christians. One of the best-known American evangelists published a 'Ten-point plan for happiness'. He started with 'Love and be loved', forgetting that Jesus said, 'You shall be hated for My name's sake.' The evangelist went on: 'Guard your health.' How can you do that when you belong to the 60% of the world that is undernourished? He said: 'Keep a sense of humour.' How can those who are being tortured for their faith keep their sense of humour? Again: 'Appreciate nature.' This advice is given when many Christians are in underground jails where they never see the sun.

But there are other, humble Christians whose chains of gold have modest studs, perhaps of even less value than silver ones. Their names are not well known in the world, but they have proved to be heroes in times of great tribulation.

It is reported from China that a Christian in Manchuria protested at the Communists' indiscriminate killings. He was dragged into a people's court and accused of crimes against the people. Then the judge ordered those watching to march past him, beating him with clubs until he died. But the people refused, declaring, 'He is a good man.'

Changing tactics, the judge promised the man freedom if he would renounce Jesus. 'Which do you choose,' he demanded, 'Jesus Christ – or Communism?'

'Jesus, Jesus, Jesus!' the Christian shouted back.

Then they took him to the riverbank for execution, and on the way he sang 'Jesus loves me' and the twenty-third Psalm set to Chinese music. He was shot in the back, but instead of falling forward on his face to grovel in the dust as victims usually do, he fell backwards, as if falling into the arms of Jesus. Reportedly the entire community was stirred by his testimony.[2]

The name of this martyr is unknown in the Free World. He had lived in humility, and that is how he died. God so ordered it that the beauty of his soul should not become the object of human praise; but he is highly valued by God.

'My spikenard'

The bride says, 'While the king sits at his table, my spikenard sends forth the smell thereof' (1:12). When the King enters the soul, the bride, like Mary of old, anoints the feet of the Bridegroom with a pure nard of gratefulness and adoration, and the world is filled with the perfume of the nard.

Nard or spikenard is made from a very small and despised plant. The fragrance from this plant comes from its root being trodden on or otherwise bruised. So, in the Church, the spiritual nard spreads its perfume only when it is bruised under the burden of the Cross.

The bride's spikenard sends forth its aroma only as long as the King sits at his table. As soon as Jesus ceases to be in your soul, the nard's fragrance disappears and the believer can no longer bring the good aroma of God to the world.

A Russian Orthodox priest named Dudko had been in jail for eleven years because he had preached what is in the Bible. His enemies nearly succeeded in killing him in a faked car accident. He continued without fear.

A Russian Christian named Orlov was imprisoned for his faith. He was fed on salted herrings and so would become very thirsty. But his captors would allow him a drink only eight hours later. Also he was not allowed to go to the lavatory when he needed it. I myself have spent fourteen years in Communist prisons, so I know what terrible torture this is. Treat yourself as he was treated, for a few hours. Then you will know what your brothers and sisters suffer.

The Russian Orthodox priest, Dudko, was re-arrested, after a period of liberty. This time he cracked and denied his convictions publicly on television. Orlov remained steadfast. Yet not only Orlov, but Dudko also served Christ! His sermons, and the books he wrote before he broke, have remained; and they continue to spread the perfume of Christ.

'A bundle of myrrh'

The bride says, 'A bundle of myrrh is my well-beloved unto me; he shall lie all night betwixt my breasts' (1:13). Every word in this verse is full of significance. The Saviour is called, 'my well-beloved'. It has sometimes been asked whether Christianity is compatible with one political doctrine or another. Christianity is compatible with nothing! For Juliet, nothing else counted except Romeo. She never talked about anything else. He was the Beloved, the only one. So, too, Jesus should be our only Beloved.

It is remarkable that the bride says, 'A bundle of myrrh is my beloved *unto me.*' No matter what Jesus might be for others, the bride says what he is for her. The apostle Thomas calls him '*My* Lord and *my* God.' No matter what he might be for others, for me he is Lord and God.

On one occasion the disciples told Jesus what men were saying about him – that he was John the Baptist, Elias, Jeremias or one of the prophets. But then Simon Peter added what Jesus was for him: 'You are the Christ, the Son of the livng God' (Matthew 16:14–16).

The bride calls Jesus 'a bundle of myrrh' – a bundle rather than a single stalk, because she found in him a multitude of qualities. There is no word in Hebrew for the English 'face' in the singular. You can only say *panim*, which means 'faces'. When the Bible says 'Seek the face of God,' it does so only in our translations. How easily believers of different Christian confessions would come to peace with one another if they would only realize that each believer has seen just one of the many faces of God, and that his brother has seen a different face! That is how they arrived at different convictions. The convictions do not exclude one another. Jesus is a bundle of myrrh; and it may be that the different confessions have each seen a different stalk.

In Communist countries Christians of many confessions suffer persecution. In Rumania the Orthodox priest, Calciu, Pitaru, a Christian from the Brethren assembly, Traian Dorz, from the Army of the Lord, the Pentecostal, Shamu, the Seventh-Day Adventist, Dragomir and the Catholic priest Godo all suffered in prisons and psychiatric asylums. They did not quarrel with one another there. They knew that Jesus is for them a *bundle* of myrrh.

The bundle which the bride keeps between her breasts is of myrrh, a plant with a bitter taste. Even if he brings her through fears and difficulties, she makes a place for him between her breasts. In the Orient women used to carry litle bags of perfume there. The bride has replaced this bag with the sufferings he allows her to experience. They are dear to her. Theirs is the fragrance she likes best.

Between her breasts

She considers that the best place for the bundle of myrrh is between her breasts. Well-educated men do not usually speak or write easily about women's breasts. Some people have been offended because this book uses erotic imagery. Because of its erotic vocabulary the Song of Songs has been greatly misused. Rabbi Akiba, who died around 135 AD, cursed those who sang this song in taverns. It must have been a common happening, or he would not have needed to pronounce the curse. The Syrian theologian, Theodore of Mopsuestia in Cilicia (350–428), considered the Song of Solomon a worldly, obscene poem without dignity, allegedly written by King Solomon to defend his marriage to an Egyptian. But the Fifth Ecumenical Synod of 553 condemned Theodore and all his writings. Later the humanist theologian, Sebastian Castellio (1515–1563), was forced to leave Geneva because he had called Solomon's Song a worldly work. However, the Church has always insisted that it is a holy book, and has explained it allegorically.

We should not be offended at the mention of women's breasts. I can see no reason why the Creator of the breasts of women should not inspire a biblical author to write about them! The breasts are the prominent part of a woman's body. Jesus finds his rest between a believer's most prominent virtues. He expects all his disciples to be prominent in some way. He asks them, 'What do you do more than others?' (Matthew 5:47). Millions said of the works of Jesus, 'Never have such things been seen.' 'Never man spoke like this man' (John 7:46). It should be possible to say the same of us. We must be prominent through fearless self-sacrifice, offering our own lives for the salvation even of our worst enemies. We must risk our lives even for the wicked, we must put them at stake in order to do any good at all.

We will see at the end of the Song the concern expressed by the believers over the fact that they have a little sister who has no breasts. They ask themselves, 'What shall we do for our sister?' (8:8). Pastors of churches must be preoccupied about souls that do not become prominent through a gift. God speaks with satisfaction of the virgin of Israel, saying of her, 'Your breasts are fashioned' (Ezekiel 16:7). This means, in spiritual language, 'You have become remarkable through exceptional deeds.' Exceptional deeds are a pleasant resting place for God in a human soul.

The words 'all night' in verse 13 in the Authorized Version do not exist in the Hebrew. The correct text is, 'He shall lie between my breasts' – period. Read it again – it could not say 'all night'. Where he is, there *is* no night.

'A cluster of camphire'

The bride says, 'My beloved is unto me as a cluster of camphire in the vineyards of En-gedi' (1:14). Camphire is a kind of perfume reminiscent of the perfume of the grapes of En-gedi. It is interesting that the name of the plant, *kopher*, is also the Hebrew word for 'atonement'. The Jews used to give the name 'cluster' to men who possessed all the virtues and all the excellences.

The Jewish teachers in ancient times divided the first word in the expression, *Eshkol kopher*, 'a cluster of camphire,' so arriving at *Ish kol kopher*, 'a man who covers all', or 'atones for all' – a fitting name for the Messiah. The most costly perfume which Jesus spreads about him is the fragrance of atonement for all sins through his sacrifice.

The author of the Song of Songs, contemplating the Saviour, remembers the vineyards of the En-gedi region. In Hebrew *En-gedi* means 'the source of the goats'. The region was so called because many wild goats lived in it. It was the region to which Solomon's father, King David, took flight when fleeing from his rival Saul, who pursued him to En-gedi but fell into the hands of David. It would have been easy for the latter to have taken revenge, but he forgave his adversary. When Solomon, David's talented son, reached maturity, a sentiment of piety led him to visit various historic scenes of his father's miraculous rise from the position of a shepherd to that of a glorious king of Israel.

A serpentine route descends with difficulty from the Judean deserts to this land through rocks and stones, eventually arriving at a little river which makes its way to the Dead Sea amidst rich vegetation and beautiful vineyards. David the fugitive would have refreshed himself with these grapes. Recalling his visit there, Solomon puts in the mouth of the bride a comparison between the Saviour and a grape of En-gedi. He also refreshes and gladdens the heart, and gives new life to the oppressed and persecuted of this world.

Jesus warned his disciples, 'They will persecute you' (John 16:20). In this respect we all share King David's fate and we all need the comfort of the Saviour. Fifteen Roman emperors strove to eradicate the Christian faith from the world, using torture to intimidate the believers. Tender maidens and children received atrocious treatment.

Saint Agnes and Saint Priscilla, both thirteen years old, were torn by metal hooks, roasted on grills and crowned with red-hot helmets. In the persecution by Diocletian, 17,000 Christians were slain in a single month. In Egypt alone 144,000 of them were put to death and another 700,000 sent into exile. The total death toll reached 11,000,000, which means 30,000 a day.

But the extent of the slaughter did not bring panic to those Christians who survived, because they had the comfort of the vineyards of En-gedi, just as persecuted David had. Amidst the torment they retained their joy and their calm, so that Augustine wrote, 'Every one of them seemed to be two people – one, somebody who suffers greatly, and also somebody who speaks words of gladness, of wisdom and of praising the Lord.' This is why the blood of the martyrs became the seed of the Church; it caused the Church to grow.

In the sixteenth century hundreds of Christians in Japan died for their faith. Some were roasted over slow fires or cut to pieces. Others had their flesh torn with pincers. The necks of some were sawed through, little by little, over a period of a week, until they finally died. Others were buried alive or were frozen to death. But all these, too, enjoyed the grapes of the mystical vineyards of En-gedi.

While she was being buried alive, the Japanese Christian Tecla, held a three-year-old girl in her arms and encouraged her to meet death with the hope of paradise. A boy of nine opened his collar himself to offer his neck to the guillotine. A boy of five, woken from sleep by the executioner's henchmen, proudly dressed in his finest clothes and was carried in the executioner's arms to the place of death; he also offered his head to the beheading block.

No Christian is alone during his tribulation; no-one is left without comfort. Just before Betty and John Stam were captured to face martyrdom at the hands of Communist soldiers in the Anwhei Province of Red China, John Stam wrote to his father: 'We're now in dangerous territory, but we're not afraid. The enclosed poem exactly expresses our feelings.' The poem was by E.U.G. Hamilton, written at the time of the martyrdom in China of the missionary Vinson:

> *Afraid? Of what?*
> *To feel the spirit's glad release?*
> *To pass from strain to perfect peace,*
> *The strife and strain of life to cease?*
> *Afraid – of that?*
>
> *Afraid? Of what?*
> *Afraid to see the Saviour's face,*
> *To hear His welcome, and to trace,*
> *The glory beam from wounds of grace?*
> *Afraid – of that?*
>
> *Afraid? Of what?*
> *A flash – a crash – a piercèd heart;*
> *Darkness – light – Oh, Heaven's art!*
> *A wound of His a counterpart!*
> *Afraid – of that?*

'Doves' eyes'

The Bridegroom says, 'Behold, you are fair, my love, you are fair; you have doves' eyes' (1:15). How strange is our relationship with our Bridegroom. Usually brides think of themselves as beautiful. Not the bride of Jesus. She says about herself, 'I am black, I did not keep the vineyards of my beauty.' In our union, it is the Bridegroom who convinces us that we are beautiful. He tells us, 'Behold, you are fair, my love; behold, you are fair.'

If he considers my soul to be beautiful, why should I worry about him ever rejecting me? We are beloved by him for our beauty. Holiness is always beautiful. Because of it we are beloved, even when we are greatly tempted, even if for a time we fall. Even if all men forsake us, we will be loved by him to the very end. He says, 'Behold, you are fair.' The bride is inclined to brood upon her blackness. He wishes us to know ourselves as he sees us – as beautiful. Humility is good only if it is a balanced humility. To overcome any doubt in us, he repeats himself: 'You are fair . . . you are fair.'

The attributes in us which especially attract Jesus are our doves' eyes. He said, '*If* . . . your eye is clear, your whole body shall be full of light' (Matthew 6:22). Whoever has clean eyes will be beloved by Jesus. The eyes should not even look towards evil; they should not be attracted by sin. They should betray no lust; they should not see the straw in someone else's eyes. They should be open to the glory of God and to the heavenly beauties. The bride has doves' eyes. Doves are chaste and faithful to their mates.

Oleg Miliutin, a Russian Orthodox, was six times committed to psychiatric institutions for openly declaring his Christian faith. He was gagged and beaten and put in a straight-jacket. He did not yield.

Khrapov, of the underground Soviet Baptist Church, resumed his evangelistic work after twenty years' confinement. A second eight-year term of imprisonment followed and then another. He died in jail, as an unbroken child of God, having spent a total of thirty-four years suffering for Christ. For a time he had led the underground Baptist Church while in hiding. Then he wrote a book which has the amazing title, *The Happiness of a Sacrificed Life*.

He had doves' eyes. He had no bitter words for torturers or traitors. He looked on life with good eyes. There are so many beautiful things to think about, and his book speaks about them. Christ loves such souls greatly.

Not only the eyes but also the whole nature of the faithful soul is that of a dove. A dove will not sit on the green branch, will not drink fresh water, will not seek shade and will avoid the company of other birds until it finds its companion. So also is the bride of Christ, so long as she is separated from her Bridegroom.

On the green bed or in the house

The bride says, 'Behold, you are fair, my beloved, yea, pleasant: also our bed is green.' The Bridegroom replies, 'The beams of our house are cedar, and our rafters of fir' (1:16–17). The bride, inebriated with happiness because of the loving words which have been spoken to her, says, 'You are fair, my beloved, yea, pleasant.' He is fair *and* pleasant. Many males are handsome but not pleasant; many are pleasant but not handsome. Jesus has both qualities.

Then she invites him, saying, 'Our bed is green.' In the midst of nature, among the blooming of lilies and the chirping of birds, upon the green grass which is a witness to the care of God towards his creatures, there the faithful soul wishes to give Jesus her love. She calls the bed, 'our bed', and he will call the house, 'our house'. Between the bride and Jesus there is a community of goods – everything which is hers is his; everything which is his is hers.

The people of Israel knew Solomon's Song, but when Jesus once commanded them to sit on the grass, they did not remember the Scripture. They ate on the grass; their hunger was satisfied; but they did not give him their love. At picnics today on the green grass there's plenty to eat and drink and we too fail to give him our love.

The Bridegroom puts forward an alternative to the green bed. The house of cedar wood is durable and does not rot. The rafters there are of fir, a fine wood used in palaces. In the Sermon on the Mount Jesus invites those who belong to him to enter into the closet (Matthew 6:6). There, in quiet, we shall enjoy the love of God.

Christians can enjoy communion with him not only in nice homes, but also in prison cells. A Soviet prisoner wrote:

> When I entered jail, in mockery I was given gigantic shoes and clothes twice my size. The sleeves reached my knees. I looked like a clown or scarecrow. When I entered the barracks, the criminals, incited by the camp commander, greeted me with laughter and ridicule.
>
> A prisoner bowed, in fake piety. 'I greet you, holy Father; you are the ambassador of Christ Himself. Do you represent the interests of heaven?'
>
> The mocking words gave me courage. Forgetting how I looked, I told them I indeed represented heaven, for which the atheists imprisoned me. While preaching to those despising sinners, the sermon affected me too. I wanted to embrace them for having reminded me of my high calling.
>
> Many fear suffering. In the past I, too, feared. But the presence of the Lord in jail has given me so many happy experiences that I would not have changed them for years of easy living in freedom.

This man has known the discreet embraces of Jesus not in a house of cedar wood, but in a Communist prison cell.

Chapter 2

Before going on to the second chapter, there are a few general considerations to be made concerning Solomon's Song. Origen, who died around 253 AD, really began the Christian allegorical interpretation of this book. Later a Mariological interpretation was devised by Ambrose (339–397), in which the bride of the Song was considered to be prophetic of Mary. From then on, commentaries either chose between these two possibilities or combined them.

As I have already said, the Church took very harsh action against those who considered the Song of Songs to be an ordinary worldly book. The Song contains not only religious teaching but also a very simple human message. Any young man who cannot love a girl wholeheartedly, and any girl who cannot love a man passionately, is not yet ready to be a marriage partner. And with such an attitude they will not be able to properly love their friends, their parents or their children.

The Song teaches a healthy attitude towards sex. Whoever is ashamed to think about sex ought also to be ashamed of the woman who gave him or her birth or of the child whom he fathers or the babe to whom she gives birth. Most of all, such people ought to be ashamed of their own sexuality. There is nothing wrong in sexual life, just as there is nothing wrong in any bodily function. Jesus had a body with all the organs and instincts we have, only he was never dominated by sin. God has ordained sexual life; he wills that there should be love between the sexes. The *Zohar* says: 'Sexual pleasure with your wife is a religious pleasure, and one which gives joy to God, too. Performed with gladness, the religious duty of conjugal intercourse, in the presence of God's glory [the *Shekinah*], gladdens your wife for the sake of the honour of the heavenly partner.'

We should not be offended that there is so much carnal love in the Song of Solomon. The body as well as the soul is created after the image of God. Our creed says that the body will be resurrected as well as the soul. Orthodox mystics speak about 'the holy flesh', because the flesh will have a part in resurrection. Jesus loved not only the souls of men, but their flesh too. Why should he not speak of the bodily charms of his bride? Justin the Martyr wrote, 'If the flesh were to be useless, why did Christ heal it? Why did He resurrect the dead? When He resurrected Lazarus and the young man in Nain and the young girl, He resurrected them soul and body.'

Solomon wrote 1,005 songs (1 Kings 5:12). Only one has remained; it is probably the most beautiful. Film actors often perform before the cameras for six or seven hours a day to produce only two or three minutes of film. Very little of what we produce in life is of high value and will endure, but it is worthwhile to write a thousand songs in order that one might be a masterpiece. We witness to many about Christ; we do many works for his kingdom. Very few of these activities have any lasting result. But those few are worth all the effort.

A carpenter witnessed to me about Christ. He died knowing that he had brought only my wife and me to faith. But we brought others to Christ; those, again, brought others; those again, others. The result is that there are now Hebrew Christian churches in Haifa, Tel-Aviv and Jerusalem which have as their true founder that carpenter. He witnessed to many without result, but he brought one to Christ who brought others, and those others brought others. Some of them became interested in helping the persecuted Christians in Communist countries. That is how a Christian mission to the Communist world began.

A little-known preacher, Mordecai Ham, brought to Christ a young boy whose name was Billy Graham. Billy Graham in his turn brought thousands upon thousands to Christ. Mordecai Ham may have witnessed to many people. He may not have had big results. But one of those won by him was exceptional. He was Ham's Song of Songs. I would encourage you to write many songs. One of them will be your Song of Songs.

Finally, we should note that in the Song, the Bridegroom is sometimes called a king, and the bride a queen. Sometimes he is a shepherd; sometimes they are workers in the vineyard. Sometimes they are in a palace; sometimes in the field. This teaches that people of all social classes are called to participate in spiritual life at the highest level.

'I am the rose of Sharon'(2:1)

Jewish commentators agree that the subject of these words is God's chosen people. Christian commentators are divided; some attribute them to the Saviour, others to the Church. What good does the debate achieve?

Only one reality exists: Godhead, which for the sake of expediency we divide into a 'He' and an 'I'. Pronouns have no place in real religious life. They are only for everyday usage. Jeremiah writes, 'This is his name whereby *he* shall be called, *The Lord* Our Righteousness' (Jeremiah 23:6). But he also writes, 'And this is the name wherewith *she* shall be called, The *Lord* Our Righteousness' (Jeremiah 33:16). Who is 'Jehovah our Righteousness?' Is it God? Is it his Church? Foolish questions. When we sit with the Father and the Son on His throne as it is promised to us (Revelation 3:21), who will be able to make a distinction then?

Nothing in the Hebrew corresponds to the 'am' in the words 'I am'. The verb 'to be' is little used in Hebrew. To understand what that means, one has to try to read the Song of Songs omitting words such as 'have', 'has', 'am', 'is', and 'are'.

Nothing 'is'; everything changes. Heraclitus said, 'Nobody can bathe twice in the same river.' Neither can anybody say of Jesus what he is. 'He has no form' (Isaiah 53:2). The rose of Sharon evokes him – but so do a lamb, a shepherd, the lion of Judah, a piece of bread in Communion. He is king, judge, high priest, victim, bridegroom, vine, brother.

The removal of the word 'is' from one's religious vocabulary saves one from the sin of judging. Nobody is *only* a bad man or a criminal, just as nobody is *only* a dentist. The dentist is also a father or mother; a Briton or Indian; a twentieth-century person; a Christian or Buddhist; a Socialist or Conservative; a virtuous or bad man, and so on. The word 'is' fixes a person to a single attribute. Life is not like that. No crook is *only* a crook. He can also be a man full of remorse, an incipient saint. No apostle is *only* an apostle; he can also be a lover of money, a trait which will transform him into a Judas. Hebrew, the language of Solomon's Song teaches us to think without the verb 'to be'.

The flowers

'I am the rose of Sharon and the lily of the valleys' (2.1) Jesus compares himself to flowers. He also compares his bride to a lily (verse 2). He says that he is like a rose. The rose is distinguished from all other flowers by the fact that it blooms in different climates and different soils. So Jesus is present in many countries, in many climates, in liberty and in persecution, in poverty and in abundance, in sickness and in health.

Roses exist in a great many colours – white, pink, purple, violet, black. The souls who reflect Jesus are also very different, and belong to different religious denominations. Only blue roses, having the colour of heaven, do not exist. So we do not have to be excessively sad about the fact that we are not yet fully heavenly! There has never yet been a blue rose. Let us strive onward, without despairing because of our weakness.

To the Greeks, the rose was a plant of love, consecrated to the goddess Venus. Comparing himself to just such a rose, Jesus is telling us that he is a lover.

The Hebrew word translated 'lily' is *havatzelet*. This is a particular flower called by botanists *colchicum autumnale* or *filius ante patrem* ('the son before the father') because it has the distinctive characteristic of blossoming before its leaves appear. The *havatzelet* is a symbol of men whose character is the opposite of those Jesus meant when he cursed the fig-tree which had rich foliage but no fruit. Those men are hypocrites, having much self-advertisement and an appearance of religion, but without its love and joy. Jesus is *filius ante patrem*. With him, and with those who belong to him, the fruits come first and the leaves afterwards.

Havatzelet is a flower which you find in Israel at every step; a flower without much outward beauty; a fitting symbol for the one who came into this world having divested himself of his divinity, living as a humble servant. The saints of God are also humble like Jesus, without added ornamentation. They are also like *havatzelet*.

The Christian Mission to the Communist World operates in Red China. Its co-workers there accept only used clothing and minimal salaries. They explain: 'Otherwise, we might become attached to things.' One of them spent many years in jail working ten hours a day barefoot in an iron mine, because she had written music for the Gospel of Luke. I heard a tape of her first song after she was released from jail. It was like hearing an angel's song. Now she gathers 300 ladies together every Sunday. The leader of the Underground Church in that region sometimes covers 800 miles by bicycle to visit all the groups. But these Christians do not wish their names to be made known, and they refuse every small amenity of life. They accept only the simplest things.

Shir-Hashirim-Rabba, an old Jewish commentary on the Song of Songs, explains Jesus' comparison of himself with a lily of the valleys thus: 'As the lily withers when it is burned by the sun, but flourishes when it is wetted by the dew, the same Israel withers, as long as it lives in the shadow of Esau; but in the future world when the shadow of Esau will have disappeared, it will be full of sap.' Hosea writes, 'I will be as the dew unto Israel: he shall grow as the lily' (Hosea 14:5).

Pliny says of the lily, 'It has a weak body which is not adequate to bear the weight of the head.' In the same way, the Church is slender and weak. Christ is too big for her. He has to bend like the head of the lily because of this.

Jesus tells us he is 'the lily *of the valleys*'. I myself have had a beautiful encounter with him in the deep valleys of suffering. When I was in solitary confinement in a Communist prison, without a Bible, I prayed that the Lord might speak to me directly. Then I heard his voice asking me, 'What is your name?' I had always known that my name was Richard. But I could not say this to Jesus, because I knew about another man who had borne this name.

Saint Richard was a Christian who lived in times of persecution. He was sentenced to death for his faith. When he was on the gallows, the hangman had some difficulty fixing the noose of the rope. Richard bowed. 'I am a farmer, and skilled in these matters,' he said gently. 'Please allow me to help you'. The hangman responded courteously and allowed Richard to attend to it.

After fixing the noose he thanked the executioner for his kindness, assured him that he bore him no grudge, and so died.

I did not have the courage to tell Jesus I bore the name of such a saint, because I was so unlike him.

We all bear beautiful names, names as Mary, Paul or John, of which we are not worthy because we are not immaculate, zealous or loving like those who bore those names before us. So I bowed before Jesus and said, 'I have no name. I long to bear yours.' To renounce the self and allow Christ to be your personality is the secret of a victorious life.

Jesus does not put such questions to you, nor does he stir you up to see their seriousness, except in deep valleys; and it is only in deep valleys that he unites himself with you to take your place, so that you in your turn might become a lily, even as he is.

Thorns and daughters

The Bridegroom says, 'As the lily among thorns, so is my love among the daughters' (2:2). God and his people pay each other the most beautiful compliments. Israel tells his Creator: 'Who is like unto you, O Lord, among the gods? Who is like you, glorious in holiness, fearful in praises, doing wonders?' (Exodus 15:11). Here God tells Israel that in his eyes she is a beautiful flower. He does not compare her to the rose which has thorns, but only to the lily which has none. Most souls are like thorns, without value or use. They prick, like the thorns in Jesus' crown. In the end, they will be burned. But not all souls persist in evil; amid the thorns there are roses.

The Bridegroom has among the girls one who is his own beloved; and, just as when he was crucified on Golgotha near a garden, the flowers remained faithful to him, sending their perfume to the cross to refresh him, so now the lily-shaped soul of his bride is his comfort and his source of strength.

Beautiful as lilies

Jesus teaches us to look closely at spiritual believers, and learn from them. He said in the Sermon on the Mount, 'Consider the lilies of the field, how they grow; they toil not, neither do they spin: and yet I say unto you, that even Solomon in all his glory was not arrayed like one of these' (Matthew 6:28–29). Those who have the happiness of finding teachers whom God sends, grow beautifully; the teachers' own secret consists of 'feeding the kids beside the shepherds' tents' (1:8). The Scripture says that Jesus has given some to be our bishops; others, pastors; others, evangelists; others, teachers who will help us to grow in all respects. They give us to be 'in Jesus'. In Him, the whole building of the Church grows to become a holy temple of God.

Christians who suffer in Communist prisons for the Holy Faith are examples of how we ought to live and are good teachers for us. A Christian named V. Petkus, was tried in a Communist court in Soviet Lithuania. No friend was allowed to attend. Petkus refused to take any part in the trial. Guards had to drag him forcibly into the courtroom. He would not accept an attorney and would not speak a single word in his own defence (neither would I, when I stood trial). The charge which was manufactured against him was a base one. Like Joseph in the Old Testament who was, though innocent, sent to jail under the accusation of attempted rape, so Petkus was charged with homosexuality because he gathered young men together in his home to teach them the faith.

We have not become like the lilies yet; therefore we protest loudly whenever the slightest harsh word is said against us. On the other hand, Petkus was happy because Jesus loved him, Jesus knew him, Jesus appreciated him. He did not say one single word to prove that what was said about him by evil men was untrue.

It is a habit of the Communists to invent numerous charges against believers. Sister Arbutenko was charged with ritual murder; Solzhenitsyn, with incest; the Bulgarian Pentecostal pastors Ladin and Haralan Popov, with counter-revolutionary spying activities and the arrest of Communists under the old regime. The Hungarian Cardinal Mindszenty had allegedly speculated in foreign currency – I, too, was accused of similar crimes. A group of Baptists in Russia received jail sentences because it was claimed that they had plotted to spread disease among the population by baptising people in the same river, giving Communion with the same cup and giving each other the holy kiss.

Although fools may have believed such accusations spread by evil men, the lily-shaped saints did not defend themselves. Their purity spoke for itself. Those who knew Brother Petkus said as much before the court: 'We know him to be a good Christian and an honest man. We have nothing else to declare. We believe like him, and have done the same things. If they are considered wrong, we too should be prisoners like him.' They answered no questions. Outside, many young people sang for hours in the street. Petkus was sentenced to ten years of prison, plus five years of deprivation.

Under his shadow

The bride says, 'As the apple tree among the trees of the

wood, so is my beloved among the sons. I sat down under his shadow with great delight, and his fruit was sweet to my taste' (2:3). We desire to sit down under his shadow. When it is very hot, one finds great comfort in sitting in the shadow of a tree. The angel told the virgin, 'the power of the Highest shall overshadow thee' (Luke 1:35). She, too must have sat in this shadow with great delight. At the time of the apostles, it was a great privilege for men that the shadow of Peter should pass over them because they were healed by it. Similarly it is happiness for us to sit in the shadow of Jesus, especially in the shadow of Golgotha, where he obtained for us the forgiveness of our sins by dying for us.

It is said of St Jerome that he always studied and wrote in the shadow of a large cross. Once he was asked why he did so. He replied, 'This tree of life gives me a shadow which shades me from all evil; it gives me fruit to strengthen me in everything which is good. I desire to spend my whole life in its shadow, and I long that its fruit should always nourish my soul.'

The important thing is that one should not push oneself to the fore. The Virgin, when overshadowed by the Holy Spirit, remained in the shadows. Most martyrs for Christ remain in the shadows. They are anonymous. Their names will never be known on earth.

Frankfurter Allgemeine, the West German newspaper, announced on 17 October 1978 that in Ethiopia, Communists sew up the eyes of Christian prisoners or gouge them out. It might well be expected that in such extremities of terror, every Christian activity would cease. In the Free World, the slightest setback is sometimes enough to discourage us from church activity. How much more then, in situations of fear, where the flesh recoils before the prospect of appalling pain or death under torture, might one expect the Christians to give up. However, in Ethiopia just the reverse happened. Christians whose names are unknown to anybody in the

Free World – who remain in the shadows so that Jesus might shine – are busy with Bible distribution as never before. They spread the Scriptures, knowing that they might be dipped in burning oil as a result of doing so.

Let us, also, sit down in the shadow of the apple tree. There we will see that its fruit which represents the Word of God, is sweet to our taste. As Psalm 119:103 says, 'How sweet are thy words unto my taste! Yea, sweeter than honey to my mouth!'

The banqueting house

The bride says, 'He brought me to the banqueting house, and his banner over me was love' (2:4). The Church is a banqueting house. God brings us into this happy place, into which we would not otherwise have come. The soul which was satisfied to sit quietly in his shadow is now brought to greater joys. In his banqueting house we will know what it means to become inebriated with his love. He has prepared for us not merely meals but banquets, with meat, milk and wines available without payment.

The great mystics and saints can be our guides towards this banqueting house. Their examples teach us that, when the Holy Spirit enters into a heart and there for the first time ignites the fire of love, that fire gives birth to an insatiable thirst. Then the believer says, 'As the hart pants after the water brooks, so pants my soul after thee, O God' (Psalm 42:1). As the hart's thirst is even greater when pursued, so is the believer's thirst for God under temptation. The thirsty hart plunges his whole body into the water and drinks his fill; we must eat and drink our fill in God's banqueting house.

St John of the Cross wrote, 'May we forget about ourselves. When we are intoxicated by his presence, we will feel that we can do miracles, that we can pass through fire and water, and that we can remain unafraid when thousands of swords are drawn against us. By his grace, we won't fear anymore – neither life nor death, joy nor sorrow. We will be drunk with faith.

This is called 'jubilation'. Sometimes you smile, sometimes you weep, and sometimes you sing. Those rational people who have no idea what the Holy Spirit does with those who belong to him ask, 'How can you be so mad?' Our reply is, 'God has permitted us to drink in his banqueting house!' But they cannot understand such a thing. The soul who has been in God's banqueting house knows unspeakable joy. He rejoices even for the pain he must endure. Whatever is done to him, however well or ill he fares, he is always peaceful and joyous. Rivers of living water flow from his heart.' Saint John of the Cross sang:

> I drank from my well-beloved
> and when I walked out,
> I knew nothing more
> of this whole field;
> and I had lost the flock
> which I had followed before.
>
> My soul has put itself,
> with all its resources,
> into His service.
> Now I have no flock anymore;
> I have no duties anymore
> Because my whole duty consists in loving.

The banner of love

As conquerors hoist their flag over conquered cities, Jesus

hoists his flag over the souls he has conquered. It is a unique flag, a flag of love. 'His banner over us is love.' It is a persistent, unvarying love. He longs to see this love expressed in the way we behave towards one another.

The famous Egyptian hermit, St Macarius, once asked God what degree of holiness he had attained after several years of fasting, prayer, solitude and sacrifice. He fell asleep, and an angel appeared to him and told him that he was still far from having reached the degree of holiness which had been attained by a certain pair of women, and that he should learn from them a better way.

Macarius went into town and found the women. They were not nuns; just ordinary housewives. 'What is the secret of your holiness?' he asked them. They wondered at the question. They were very busy caring for their husbands and their several children. They had little time to pray. Because of the amount of work they had to do, they often missed church. They were illiterate and so could not read Holy Scripture. They were simple-minded and could not meditate much. They were as they described themselves: 'poor wives amidst constant worldly cares'.

Macarius continued to make enquiries about them and discovered that they were married to two brothers. They lived together under the same roof, not once quarrelling, or permitting harsh words to pass between them. From this St Macarius learned that living together in love, passing through all frictions without ever saying a harsh word or throwing a harsh look, can be more graceworthy in the eyes of God than a great deal of fasting and prayer. The banner over us is love.

In the Jilava prison in Rumania, several prisoners were put naked into a cell without beds, without blankets and without a barrel to serve as a lavatory. They were never allowed to leave their cell to fulfil their bodily needs. Imagine passing the night, completely naked, in such a stinking cell.

One of the prisoners was sick with pulmonary

tuberculosis. Late one night, he could not bear to stand on his feet any longer. He fell, and would have frozen to death on the cold concrete, had not the Christian Mircea Vulcanescu, used all his powers of persuasion to convince the sick man that he, Vulcanescu, was perfectly healthy. Therefore he would stretch himself out on the concrete and the sick man would then be able to seat himself on his body and have the protection of his bodily warmth.

Vulcanescu's insistence was so great that the sick man could not resist indefinitely, and he accepted. Vulcanescu remained stretched out naked on the concrete while the sick man slept for a few hours. He too fell asleep. When they awoke, Vulcanescu was almost frozen. The other prisoners had spent the entire night moving around without sitting on the concrete. Vulcanescu contracted pulmonary tuberculosis himself. Soon after this he died, but he demonstrated that the Saviour's banner over us is love.

In Florence, in Italy, the Red Brigade leader Furbelone planned a bank robbery – what the Brigade terms an 'expropriation'. Two revolutionaries disguised as policemen stood at the entrance to the building, while two others entered to force the teller to give up the money. A car with a false licence number waited in front of the bank to ensure the escape. Furbelone himself, disguised as a beggar, sat on the steps of the Santa Maria Church opposite the bank, from which post he was to give the signals controlling the operation.

Just as he was about to signal the start of the robbery, a little girl at her mother's side, on her way to school, ascended the steps for a short prayer. Seeing the beggar, she took her lunch out of her bag, broke off a part for herself, and gave him the remainder.

Irritated by this interruption in his plans, Furbelone intended to push the girl aside. But all at once he was struck by the thought: This is a human being who looks upon me with love, who considers me honest and worthy of esteem. Instead of giving the signal to start the robbery, the notorious terrorist took the sandwich from the smiling girl and entered the church with her. His criminal life was over.

A man does not lack possessions if he gives to the poor. This little girl obtained the double blessing of bringing a soul to Christ and of stopping a serious crime.

'Comfort me'

The bride says, 'Stay me with flagons, comfort me with apples: for I am sick of love' (2:5). The bride must be strengthened to bear the embraces of the Bridegroom. The archangel Gabriel said to the Holy Virgin, 'The power of the Highest shall overshadow you' (Luke 1:35), in order that she might bear the descent of the Holy Spirit upon her. It is written of John the Baptist that he would walk before the Saviour in the Spirit and in the power of Elijah. So we can see that we must be empowered to bear spiritual love. Showers of blessing are not easily borne.

Ezekiel says, 'The Spirit entered into me and set me upon my feet' (3:24). Saint Ephrem knew such jubilation that he cried, 'God, take your hand away from me for a little, because my heart is too weak to bear such a joy.' Saint Peter, when he saw Jesus work a miracle, fell at his feet saying, 'Depart from me; for I am a sinful man, O Lord' (Luke 5:8). A sinful man has not the power to witness the beautiful magnificence of the Lord. We who know his embraces need power. Those who pass through great suffering for his sake need power too.

In Maputo in Mozambique many Christians were jailed. Some were natives, others were from Zimbabwe, South Africa, Portugal and America. The torturer Karonga used to torment the prisoners in the following way. He ordered his soldiers to tie the hands of the prisoner tightly behind his back with string. His arms were wrenched up to the height of his chest, and then tied in such a way that if he moved at all the string would cut cruelly into his flesh. For a few minutes the prisoner sat in agony, and then the soldiers poured water into his gaping wounds and rubbed salt into them. The prisoner would roll about on the ground in absolute torment. The other prisoners were forced to sit nearby and watch. No-one was allowed to go to the victim's aid.

Prisoners were almost eaten alive by mosquitoes, lice and bedbugs. They had to work as slaves in labour camps with only three or four hours for proper sleep. Girls were raped. Sometimes prisoners were unable to wash for a month. When they insisted on being allowed to wash they were taken to a river that was full of crocodiles. There the Communists forced some of the men into the water.

In the prisons of Mozambique, we have brothers and sisters who are spreadeagled on the ground and beaten, or hung from trees by their feet. Many die from exhaustion, tetanus and snake bites. Without strength from God, they could not bear these tortures for his sake. Without strength from on high, they could not bear his embraces either.

The bride is sick of love. Her love is passionate. In the Orient, the sickness of love is much more widespread than in Europe or America. It is written of David's son, Amnon, that 'he fell sick for his sister Tamar' (2 Samuel 13:2). Men can die from this sickness. The bride asks to be stayed with flagons, a kind of pie made of the grapes which have had the juice pressed out of them. These flagons were usually brought as offerings to Ishtar, the Babylonian goddess of love. The bride also asks to be strengthened with apples. But she will soon discover that the sickness of love cannot be cured with pressed grapes or apples. It can only be cured by the presence of the Most Beloved. Our thirst for Jesus is not quenched but merely soothed by his gifts which are a foretaste of the happiness we will possess in his presence in heaven.

Don't envy the bride

We become jealous when we hear of somebody having such love as the bride's, which is so passionate that it even makes her ill. But not everyone has to have such a richness of feeling, with which also comes great responsibilities. Men are of different types. With some, the power of reasoning predominates; with others, the imaginative faculty. One will have little judgement but rich imaginative powers; another, the gift of penetrating intellect but cold emotions. It is wrong to envy what another possesses. We must consecrate to God the gifts that we possess. The Lord accepts various attitudes.

Pastor Son was imprisoned in Korea during the Japanese occupation. A guard wanted to help him, and told the prosecutor, who was questioning the pastor, 'He performs the rites at the Shinto shrines faithfully.' (The Japanese had imposed on the Korean people the obligation to bow before the image of the emperor at these shrines; they considered him to be the god of all the earth.)

If Pastor Son had only kept silent, he would have been freed. But he contradicted the guard. 'That is not so', he said. 'I have never taken part in shrine worship.'

The prosecutor was perplexed. 'It has been nearly three years since you've seen your family. Don't you want to see them? Will you not give up your obstinate ideas?'

Pastor Son replied, 'I can't give up my faith.'

'Haven't three years of suffering made any difference to you at all?'

'A Christian faith grows stronger through suffering,'

replied the pastor. 'So it has done me good to be in prison. I do not mind what happens. If I return home, Christ will be with me; and if I stay in prison, he will still be with me.'

Pastor Son's was one possible attitude in the circumstances – the attitude of a perfect lover of Jesus. On the other hand, other Christians used their reasoning powers and by giving clever answers tried to escape suffering if possible.

During World War II, Protestant Christians were greatly persecuted in Rumania, which was under Nazi domination. A preacher was brought before the police inspector. 'Do you preach love?' he asked.

The Christian replied, 'I do.'

'Do you also preach that one should love one's enemies?'

'Indeed I do. That is the teaching of Jesus.'

And now came the big question. 'Then do you also love the soldiers of the Soviet army?'

The preacher knew that if he answered 'Yes', when the Soviet army was fighting against Rumania, it would mean certain imprisonment. So he answered: 'How can you ask me whether I love the Soviet army? Our country is at war with them.'

The police inspector was very pleased. He said, 'You are a real patriot.'

During the War the services of Baptists, Adventists, Pentecostals and other denominations were forbidden in Rumania. A Christian was asked by a police inspector, 'Do you still gather for worship?' He replied, 'Christian gatherings are forbidden now.'

The inspector shook him by the hand, saying 'I am happy that you are a law-abiding citizen.'

Such Christians had not stood up clearly for the truth; neither had they told a lie. They simply used a trick, and they succeeded. Some used stratagems determined by reason, whereas the attitudes of some were dictated only by passionate love. In no circumstances would the latter compromise.

Passionate love is not the only possibile attitude towards

Christ. He receives also those who are attached to him instead by their reasoning powers.

His embrace

The bride says, 'His left hand is under my head, and his right hand does embrace me' (2:6).

In Solomon's Song, the loving bride is also wise. She knows that, according to biblical symbolism, the left side is the side of God's rigour, while the right side is the side of compassion. Therefore she lies down to the left of her Beloved, among the sinners. Putting her head upon his left arm, she immobilizes this side; she incapacitates his severity, and he has only his right hand free – the caressing hand of love.

There is great variety in the experiences of believers. The Carmelite nun, Anne of St Bartholemew (1549–1626), companion of Teresa of Avila, wrote in her biography:

> Christ the Lord appeared to me in the shape in which He walked on this earth. He was exceedingly handsome, though He seemed very sad. Approaching me, He put His right hand on my left shoulder with an unspeakable weight, which I could never explain to anybody. Thus He caused His pain and suffering to enter into my heart, and He said to me, 'Behold the souls I lose.' He challenged me to work for the salvation of souls, and showed me all France so impressively and so clearly that it was as though I were present in every place; and I saw how many millions of souls are lost. This happened in a single moment, and if it had lasted any longer I feel my life would have ended.

Christ put his hand on her to make her share his pain. It was different with the bride in the Song. He used his right hand only to embrace her.

Being thus reassured, the bride can fall asleep with his left hand under her head. Her soul is in sweet communion with Jesus; angels watch around them.

An army of roes

Her last words before falling asleep are, 'I charge you, O you daughters of Jerusalem, by the roes, and by the hinds of the field, that you stir not up, nor awake my love, till he please' (2:7). The oath is made by the roes and the hinds of the field because they are symbolic of the Beloved, and because they are timid creatures which must not be troubled when their time of love comes.

The Hebrew word for 'roes' is *sabaot*. One of God's names is *Jehovah Sabaot*, which means 'The Lord of Hosts'. So *Sabaot* means both 'roes' and 'hosts', which is very strange. It shows that God's army is an army apart. Roes are shy, timid creatures which attack nobody. They have conquered the hearts of many nature lovers, poets and painters by their beauty. God's army is like an army of roes.

But what of the many military exploits of the Jewish army under Moses, Joshua and David? Consider the Salvation Army of today. It speaks in military language. Its magazine is called *The War Cry*. The Army is composed of corps instead of churches. Instead of preachers it has officers. In its beginning, its vocabulary was entirely military. It boasted that it had 'assaulted' places of sin, that it had 'taken prisoners', and so on. The Salvation Army fights in order to bring people to peace with God.

The army of Israel is also meant to be an army of peace,

but this is a phenomenon so unique that there are no words to describe its battles. It has to speak of its works of peace in the language of men of war, in much the same way that modern microphysics continually uses the language of classical physics, even though the scientists know that that language does not describe the facts of microphysics. The physicists have not yet had time to develop a new vocabulary.

So when we read in the Bible of 'the sword of the Lord', of armed and bloodthirsty angels, of a carnage prepared by God himself, we must understand that the exploits of God's roes – unarmed, shy, loving creatures, who would rather die than attack anybody – are spoken of in military terms only because humans have no other appropriate language.

The sleep of faith

Taken literally, we have here a demand to the friends of the bride that they must not disturb the nuptial joy of the young pair during the seven days of the wedding feast. It is an unkind act to wake somebody from sleep for no good important reason. It is even worse to trouble a believing soul sleeping the quiet sleep of faith, in the protecting arms of Jesus. That soul is in communion with the Lord, and whoever prods him will get his punishment, whoever he might be.

What a wonderful sleep this is! Scripture teaches us that for the soul who sleeps trustfully, believing in the One who considers the sinner to be just, his faith; his quiet sleep is accounted as righteousness. God delights in this quiet loving sleep of faith. There is no activity which he prefers to it. Nobody is allowed to disturb the ecstasy of love. The soul must not be stirred up or awakened.

To stir up and to awake are two different things. The one who awakes only calls the sleeper, who then has to conquer sleep himself. The one who stirs him up makes a better job of it; he forces him to come out of sleep. Both are forbidden when somebody sleeps in the arms of Jesus.

Many things trouble the quiet sleep of Christian faith. In Communist countries it is troubled by the stooges of the Communists among the clergy. Bingh, the Catholic bishop of Saigon (now Ho Chi Minhville) and a Communist stooge, published the following statement in the Communist newspaper *Humanité*: 'Previously, Catholics have had strong prejudices against revolutionaries. The propaganda of the former regime presented the Communists as the destroyers of all religions. Now we have seen the reality. Our church is the victim of no persecution.' But he surely knew about the mass graves filled with the bodies of thousands of people killed by the Viet Cong in Hue and Quang Tri. He knew that his parishioners were forced to denounce one another, or else face imprisonment. He knew about the parents who had killed their children to keep them from falling into the hands of godless Communists.

Bishop Bingh knew what had happened to his own Catholics. The convents in Thu Duc were closed. Clergymen were arrested; all the monks in Mossard and the Trappists in Phuoc-Son and Phuoc-ly were jailed. They all fell asleep quietly in their prison cells, trusting in Jesus, and keeping their faith in him. It was wrong of the bishop to trouble their quiet sleep.

The Jesuit priest, H. Stephenson, after visiting China, described the Communist Chinese as 'exemplary anonymous Christians whose examples should be emulated by Western Christians. They value people above things.' It did not disturb this Jesuit that the murderers whom he calls 'anonymous Christians' have jailed or killed absolutely all the Jesuits of Red China, and many other innocent Catholics and Evangelicals besides. The bishop Kung Pin and the Protestant pastor Wan-Min-Dao have been in jail for twenty-five years.

Similar betrayals happen amongst Protestants. Pastor

V. Rumatshik, of the Soviet Baptist Underground Church, wrote:

> Unfortunately, we also have some believers who work together with the Communist authorities. This gives them the possibility of travelling abroad in order to lead foreign Christians astray in the matter of religious liberty. These preachers render the atheists a great service by hiding from the public the real situation. They make the world believe that we have much freedom without chains and oppressions. These men behave so, because they love this world; and they receive their reward on earth.

The prisoners spend their years in the quiet embrace of Jesus, sleeping faithfully on his bosom. They ought not to be troubled by such lies uttered by men of the clergy.

Do not awake love

The demand addressed to the daughters of Jerusalem also has another meaning. We must not awaken artificially the love that is in us. We must wait until it is given to us by God. God's heart must encounter our hearts. Even the false faith of another person should not be corrected by force before the time is right. That would do them more harm than leaving them temporarily in their erroneous beliefs. Allow time to do its work.

A Moslem in a Russian jail asked a Christian pastor, 'If Christianity is so great, will we have this faith after we die? Where will Muhammad, our prophet, be then?'

The pastor replied, 'Muhammad, like everyone else, will receive there according to his deeds. I do not believe God will reject him. God loves everyone'.

'Our religious leaders say that only Moslems will be saved, and that Christians and Jews will go to the devil.'

'Are you married?' asked the pastor.

'Yes, and I have children.'

The pastor continued: 'If you had three children, and two were blind, would you think of all of them as yours?'

'Of course,' answered the Moslem. 'And I would love the blind ones more than the other.'

'Similarly,' concluded the pastor, 'God loves men of all faiths. Compared to his love, ours is like a piece of ice compared to the sun. God sends nobody to hell because he belongs to another religion.' Soon the Moslem was baptised, and received appropriate instruction in the Christian faith.

Stirring up love, using brutal means to bring somebody to the true faith and exercising coercion, produce great catastrophes. There are enough evils in this world. We do not need another – artificial, unnatural, faked love.

It is terrible to awaken needs that don't exist. Why don't we wait until the needs come? Why do we stir up feelings by artificial techniques? How often this great crime is committed by religious leaders. All manner of means are employed to attract the masses!

So it comes about that men fill the churches, not because they love the Saviour, but because they are under some kind of physical or psychological compulsion. When persecution comes, it becomes obvious that these souls did not have a real love for God. Our love towards Christ must be authentic, bridal love.

Bridal love

The secret police had come to search the house of Antonii, the Orthodox bishop of Arkhangelsk. Finding the vessel used for Holy Communion, they threw it on the floor and trampled on it. The bishop threw himself across it, trying to protect it with his body. He lost consciousness. When he awoke he was in jail.

They asked his opinion about the future of the Russian Church, and wanted to know if he desired the overthrow of the Soviets. He answered that the Church would be glorified through the suffering of its martyrs, as it was in the first centuries, and that he prayed daily that the Soviet government would not shed blood and would be forgiven for its sins.

First he was threatened with death, then was promised freedom if he would become an informer for the police. The bishop was not frightened, and could not be bought. He was put in a small cell together with five others. They endured bitter cold, and received only two glasses of water a day and nothing else. They could not wash or change their clothes, and lived in their own stench. They lost their teeth. The bishop became so weak that he could not clean the invading bugs and lice out of his beard. When he felt death near he chanted his own funeral service. He died with prayers on his lips. He was an authentic bride of Christ.

Leaping upon the mountains

The bride says, 'The voice of my beloved! behold, he comes leaping upon the mountains, skipping upon the hills. My beloved is like a roe or a young hart; behold, he stands behind our wall, he looks forth at the windows, showing himself through the lattice' (2:8-9). He comes leaping upon the mountains. Difficulties mean nothing to him. He does not know discouragement. He bears for us the curse, the burden, of death on the cross; he fights the powers of darkness. He leaps over our bad deeds as well; he leaps over them as if they had never existed.

Some people doubt that our salvation can be very near, because not all the biblical prophecies about the last times have yet been fulfilled. But when Jesus returns, he will not worry about our calculations. He leaps upon the mountains.

'He stands behind our wall'

Only a wall separates us from him. This knowledge was a great comfort to prisoners in a Communist camp who were compelled to stand facing a wall for weeks.

Midrash Rabba, a rabbinical commentary on the Song, says that what is meant here is the Wailing Wall in Jerusalem, a wall from which the glory of God never departs. But we recall Job's words: 'I know that my Redeemer lives, and that he shall stand at the latter day upon the earth' (Job 19:25). Our flesh, our body, is the wall which separates the bride from the Bridegroom. He is behind this wall. After death we will be face to face with him.

For the time being he looks through the windows; sometimes one, sometimes another. He examines one side of our character, then another side, to know what stage of spiritual maturity we have reached. We, too, must be attentive to what is going on in our souls. Knowing this, St Blandine, a slave girl from Lyon, went to her death before the wild animals 'radiant with joy as if she had been invited to a wedding feast'. Saint Ignatius, bishop of Antioch, wrote, 'Let me be the fodder of the beasts, by which I might find God. Let me imitate the example of my God.' Also Origen, another celebrated teacher of the Church, said in a sermon, 'I do not doubt that in this assembly there are men known to God alone, who are already martyrs for him by the testimony of their conscience; because they are ready even now, if asked, to shed their blood for the name of Jesus Christ.'

The winter is past

Here the most beautiful part of Solomon's Song begins. What follows are words appropriate for those convicted of sin; and they are a great source of comfort for the saints when they have passed through a period of depression. They are also fitting words for the time of a believer's death: 'My beloved answered and said unto me, "Rise up, my love, my fair one, and come away. For lo, the winter is past, the rain is over and gone; the flowers appear on the earth; the time of the singing birds is come, and the voice of the turtle is heard in our land; the fig tree puts forth her green figs, and the vines with the tender grape give a good smell. Arise, my love, my fair one, and come away. O my dove, that art in the clefts of the rock, in the secret places of the stairs, let me see your countenance, let me hear your voice; for sweet is your voice, and your countenance is comely" ' (2:10–14). The bride hears the voice of her much-beloved. She does not see him, but she recognizes his voice, and is overcome by an unspoken joy.

The bride says, 'My beloved answered and said unto me' (this is the precise translation of the Hebrew). We often find this expression used elsewhere about the Lord; he is said to have answered when nobody has asked him anything. He responds to the unspoken anxieties of the heart. We should practise not only vocal but also mental prayer. Let our unspoken thoughts and affections rise up to him!

The word *anah* used here means 'to answer' and 'to sing', or, rather, 'to chant', as they do in synagogues, Orthodox churches and mosques. Solomon's Song, like the whole Hebrew Bible, contains not only text but also musical notation, indicating how it should be chanted. The *Zohar* says, 'the tonal accents were also delivered to Moses on Sinai.' This applies to the Law of Moses and also to the other books of the Old Testament. Anybody who does not know the tonal accents does not know the entire revelation of God. The same words sung in different keys stir up different feelings. This book has in truth been given to us as a song. In fact, Solomon has been described as the first composer of opera.

'In the clefts of the rock'

Believers are strong and unyielding towards sin. That is why it is written, 'Judah is like a lion's cub.' But in their relationship with God, they are like innocent and inoffensive doves, loving quiet and serenity. Like doves, they are faithful to their mate, the Bridegroom.

This dove is in its right place – in the clefts of the rock which is Christ. If she is with him, a cleft of a rock is as good as the King's chamber, a prison cell as good as a comfortable house. Jesus encourages her to have communion with Him: 'Let me hear your voice; for sweet is your voice, and your countenance is comely.' How sweet is the voice of the believer in Jesus! A Jewish commentator asks why the wives of the patriarchs Abraham, Isaac and Jacob were barren. It was because God loved their prayers, their words and their voices. God allowed them to be barren so that they would need to pray for healing from barrenness. Why do believers undergo troubles? Because to God, their voices are sweet. He desires that they should lift their voices in prayer and in song to him.

Some believers have been known to produce tremendous effects with their voices. A Christian, released not long before from a Lithuanian prison, wrote:

> My outward appearance is not attractive. In the slave labour camp, I worked underground. There was an accident which left me a hunchback. Once a boy stopped me on the street and asked, 'Uncle, what do you have on your back?' I was sure that mockery would follow, but I still replied, 'A hump.'
>
> 'No!' said the child. 'God is love, He gives deformities to nobody. You do not have a hump, but a box below your shoulders. Inside, angel's wings are hidden. One day the box will open; and with those wings you will fly to heaven.'
>
> I began to cry with joy; I am crying now, even as I write.

Such was the achievement of one Christian child's voice. Because his voice was rightly modulated, he could make a hunchback happy. Therefore the Bridegroom says, 'Let me hear your voice, for sweet is your voice.'

Cederholm, a Finnish prisoner in the USSR who eventually got free because he was a foreigner, says that in Leningrad he was put in a cell reserved for men under sentence of death. There he found, among many other inscriptions written by those who had been awaiting execution, the following words: 'In the name of the Father, and of the Son, and of the Holy Ghost, Archimandrite Anthony, of Alexandro-Nevsky monastery, is to be shot tonight for refusing to burden his conscience with a grievous sin. Forgive them, Lord, for they know not what they do. Good people, tell my brethren I leave this world with peace in my soul.' The inscriptions on the walls alternated with inscribed crosses, under which were names and dates. In the corner of the cell was an image of St Seraphim of Sarov, drawn in indelible pencil. The image was poignantly drawn by an untrained hand, but all the details were carefully done, and it was signed thus: 'Ecaterina, the servant of God, drew this image, thinking of her little children who are praying to the just God for their Mama.' How beautiful are the voices of those who speak like this!

'Sweet is your voice'

Saint Augustine wrote, 'Whoever praises God in song praises Him twice – in the words, and in the music.' Much depends on the spirit in which we sing. In the Soviet Union, there were Christians who have not owned a hymnal for decades. In Red China the same is true. With what exuberant joy they sing when hymnals are smuggled to China for them! We should sing with the same joy.

In Communist prisons, naked Christians were thrown crosswise over narrow tables. Their legs dangled from one side; from the others, the head and arms. The legs were tied to the arms with straps. One either side, Communists stood with whips and beat the prisoners until they bled. Before being beaten, they were told to sing. They could have refused, and paid for their refusal with a more savage beating. But why should they not sing, when hymns like *O Sacred Head now wounded, with grief and shame weighed down* were demanded from them?

One of those who underwent this ordeal was a Hebrew Christian. He knew the story of Rabbi Akiba, who sang while being combed with red-hot iron combs and died a martyr's death under the ordeal. Akiba's disciples asked him, 'How can you sing when you are suffering so greatly?'

He replied, 'All my life I have desired to love God with all my heart and all my soul, but I was always distracted by worldly things. Now for the first time I can praise God with all my heart.'

It was a rare privilege for that Hebrew Christian to sing such a song just before being flogged until he bled.

Let the reader imagine himself in such a situation. Let him visualize the scene, and try to sing those words himself:

O Sacred Head now wounded, with grief and shame weighed down,
Now scornfully surrounded with thorns, Thine only crown.
O Sacred Head, what glory, what bliss till now was Thine
Yet though despised and gory, I joy to call Thee mine.

Sometimes Christians were ordered to sing '*A mighty fortress is our God*', in the certain knowledge that after a few minutes they would be tortured. Nevertheless they sang that God is a trusty shield and weapon, that 'He helps us free from every need that has us now o'ertaken.' The Communists mocked them. 'Do you really believe that God will help you free from this need?' they said. Catholics sang the song, *Hail, Mary, full of grace*.

I personally went through the extremes of temptation and doubt when I passed through similar situations. I was forced to sing Psalm 121, '. . . My help comes from the Lord. He will not suffer your foot to be moved . . . He that keeps Israel shall neither slumber nor sleep. The Lord is your keeper'. We asked ourselves then 'What is the value of such words when they don't correspond in any way to the reality in which we are living?' And in that situation I had a revelation, which forever pacified my mind, however terrible the circumstances.

I thought, 'To whom are such promises made?' There was only one possible answer: 'To me, and to the "me" of every believer.' But who is this 'me'? A 'me' only has existence as an abstraction, just as pure gold or uranium are abstractions. In nature we only find ores. These have to be melted down in a furnace in order to extract one little bit of uranium or gold from huge quantities. The case is similar with the 'me' in every believer. In a soul there are so many elements which do not belong to the 'me'. They are the influences of heredity, of a poor education and of all kinds of demonic evil. Only very little of us forms the 'me', what St Teresa of Avila called 'the inner castle'.

My real personality – my uniqueness – is an image of God; it is my sanctified being, united with Christ; it is what St Peter calls 'the hidden man of the heart' (1 Peter 3:4). The promises that nothing will hurt us, that we will be protected from all harm, do not apply to the whole ore. In order that the real me should live in perfect cleanliness and holiness, the ore has to pass through cleansing fire. I know that the inner castle will not be harmed, that the God of Israel watches over it. The only part of me that matters can be at peace. No enemy will ever reach it.

Let us sing in this spirit; and then we too will hear the Bridegroom say, 'Let us hear your voice; for sweet is your voice, and your countenance is comely.' The word used in the Hebrew is actually a plural word – 'countenances'. The relaxed, serene face of a Christian at ease; the joyful face of one having a good time; the distorted face of one in pain; the marred face of one who is enduring torture; the radiant face of one in ecstasy – they are all comely in his sight.

'The little foxes'

The Bridegroom tells the bride, 'Take us the foxes, the little foxes, that spoil the vines; for our vines have tender grapes' (2:15). He does not say, 'take me', but 'take us'. Both Bridegroom and bride desire to enjoy the fruit of the vine. It is their common interest to eradicate the foxes which spoil it. All who wish to help in this task, and are capable of it, are included in this calling.

What is meant by these foxes? Firstly, they are our corruptions. Those things in us which hinder the flourishing of godly life must be set aside. Foxes are animals which often turn their heads and look back. They are usually portrayed in that attitude. It is a characteristic in us also, and one which must be reformed. Whosoever has put his hand to the plough of the Kingdom and looks back, is not worthy of Jesus. The fox is also a byword for cunning. A believer should not be devious.

Our battle is not only against major sins but also against minor ones. It is possible for the sun in all its greatness to be reflected in a mirror, even though the sun is so much larger than the earth; yet the tiniest object that interposes itself between the mirror and the sun obscures it. So our little hearts can mirror the great God; but the slightest thing can hide our hearts from him. Thomas More wrote:

> *Alas, how light a cause may move*
> *Dissension between hearts that love.*
> *Hearts that the world in vain has tried*
> *In sorrow, but more closely tied*
> *Which stood the storm when waves were rough*
> *Yet in a sunny hour fell off*
> *Like ships that have gone down at sea*
> *When heaven was all tranquillity.*

We should never underestimate the harm a small sin can do. Think what damage a tiny microbe or an invisible virus can do; they can bring about your death. So it is with sin. Little flies and ants destroy animal carcasses with astonishing speed. A swarm of ants can devour a horse's corpse as quickly as can a lion. Our vineyards are not yet in fruit; because even if they have reached great excellence, our earthly virtues are only blossoms. The fruit will not be seen until the life to come. For the time being, the vineyard is in bloom. And we must beware of foxes – even little foxes.

Let us remember that just as the soul can be devastated not only by gross sins but also by a multitude of neglected minor sins, so the life of holiness in its turn is not only composed of great heroic deeds, but also of a multitude of small actions and brief words. It is not only the miracles and the martyr deaths which have significance, but also the small deeds. It is not only the lightning which counts, but also the sunbeam; not only the powerful torrents and roaring waterfalls, but also the quiet pools of Siloam.

It matters that we should avoid small evils, refrain from little sins and minor inconsistencies and weaknesses. We should avoid foolishness and not fall into some small indiscretion or imprudence. It matters that we should resist making concessions to our self, to our earthly nature. We need to beware those fleeting moments of laziness and indecision and those small acts of cowardice. An important element of the holy life is the rejection of these things.

When the United States first launched its space shuttle, it was announced that the failure of a tiny piece of plastic, worth mere cents, had resulted in a million-dollar delay in America's space programme. A brief quarrel with a marriage partner over a trifling matter can destroy a Christian marriage, wreck the children's personalities and bring the gospel into disrepute in the neighbourhood.

Two women went to a monastery to worship. One had her conscience burdened with a great sin. The other did not regard herself as a sinner, because she had been guilty only of small things. The abbot listened to their confessions, and then sent them both to a field. He ordered the great sinner to bring the largest stone she could find. The one with only small sins was told to bring only little stones. This they did. After they had brought the stones to the abbot he said, 'Now put them back, each in the exact place you found it.'

The woman who had brought the small stones hesitated. The abbot asked her why. She answered, 'It is difficult, because there are so many, and I can't remember where they all came from.'

Then the abbot told her, 'Remember, your companion has committed just one, big, evil deed. But she remembers it, regrets it, and washes it with her tears. She knows the place from which the stone was taken. But you, with your small and unimportant sins, just like the little foxes in Solomon's Song, which spoil the vines, can't remember how or when or to whom you did wrong. And because your sins are small and numerous you may not even be able to repair them. They remain a burden on your soul, just as these little stones remain in your apron.'

Hearing these words, the woman bowed her head and acknowledged that she was no purer than her sister. She understood that she, who had committed only small sins, also needed to repent of them and be forgiven in order to purify her soul. Let us take heed of small sins.

Once two men built a wall. When one of them was placing a brick, he noticed that it was thicker in one place than another. 'Throw it away,' said his friend, 'and get another. Otherwise the results will be unsatisfactory.'

'Leave me alone,' the first man retorted. 'How can such a little thing, which nobody is going to notice, do any harm? You take things too seriously.' He continued putting one brick upon another until evening, when they finished their work and went home.

What did they see when they came to work the next day? Because of that one uneven brick, the wall had not been vertical. Because of the way it had been built, it had leaned further and further over. As a consequence it had collapsed during the night, and the work had to be done all over again. So it is with every small sin or little untruth in our hearts. A very small lie will grow and grow in us, until it brings us shame and reproach. Don't regard little sins as unimportant.

Our universe is made up of things so tiny that they cannot be seen even through the most powerful of microscopes. The diameter of the dome of St Peter's basilica in Rome is about the same measurement as the height of a fourteen-storey house. Imagine a dust particle in it. As the size of the dust particle is to that of the basilica, so (approximately) is the size of an electron compared to that of an atom. And if everything were to be increased in size so that a baseball became the size of the planet earth, then the atoms of the baseball would become the size of grapes. When the electrons and protons function normally, they sustain our lives. When they are tampered with, a town like Nagasaki disappears. It is of the greatest importance that the smallest of things should function correctly. Beware of little foxes!

Children's sins

Often we are not serious in drawing the attention of children to their sins, because they are so small. But small sins can poison a child's life. On the other hand, children who have repented of their small sins and have been purified by the blood of Christ are capable of great things for him.

In a small village school in Communist Hungary there were children who had fought their small sins and now had great faith. A new teacher arrived – a militant atheist whose objective was to root out religion from the hearts of the children.

One day she summoned little Angela – a very pious girl – and asked her, 'What do you do if your parents call you?'

'I come immediately.'

'What happens if your parents call somebody else?'

'They come, too.'

'Well,' said the teacher, 'they all come, and you come, because you really exist. But suppose your parents called your grandparents, who have been dead a long time. Would they come?'

'Surely not!'

'And if they were to call Red Riding Hood or Snow White – would they come?'

'Surely not, because they are just imaginary.'

'You see, children,' said the teacher triumphantly, 'only living beings, which actually exist, can respond to a call. If somebody doesn't come when called, he is not alive. Is that clear?'

'Yes,' replied the whole class.

The teacher sent Angela out of the classroom and told her to stand by the door. Then she said to the other children, 'Call her!' The children shouted, 'Angela! Angela!' Angela immediately entered the room.

'Now, everything is clear,' declared the teacher. 'You have all been brought up to believe in Jesus. You believe that he exists, that he is alive, and that he hears you when you speak to him. Is that so?'

'Yes.'

'Now, we will try an experiment. Angela entered the classroom when we called her. So, everybody, on the count of three shout as loudly as you can, "Come, Lord Jesus; come, Lord Jesus!" One, two, three – begin to call!'

Nobody dared to shout. The teacher laughed. 'There you have the proof. You don't even dare to call him, because you know he would not come. He *could* not come, because he is just as imaginary as Red Riding Hood or Snow White.'

Then something unexpected happened. Angela turned to the children and said, 'We *will* call Jesus! All together – Come, Lord Jesus!'

With hands folded and a deep yearning in their hearts,

with total confidence, the children began to chant, 'Come, Lord Jesus! Come, Lord Jesus!' Angela prompted them again and again: 'Come, Lord Jesus!' They shouted so loudly that it seemed as if the walls would crumble.

What happened next, according to the children's later acount, was that they saw the door opening; then a great light shone through; and then standing bathed in that light was a beautiful child, smiling at them. At the same time they heard their teacher's desparing cry. 'He has come! He has come!'

She rushed from the room, slamming the door behind her. She had to be put into an asylum; she had gone mad.

The children were rigorously cross-examined by pastors. Their accounts of what had happened did not contradict one another. This is an authentic, story.

Little children can do great things for the Lord, if they forsake their little sins!

'I am not'

The bride says, 'My beloved is mine, and I am his' (2:16). Baalshem-Tov, the founder of the Hassidic sect within Judaism, fainted whenever he read these words. For a believer, they are too much to contemplate.

But there is something even better than this peak of beauty. Male love is often selfish and ambitious to possess for itself, but our love for Jesus is of the female type – free of selfishness, persisting only in the ambition to give itself completely.

The believing soul is continually growing. Its first word is an exclamation of triumph. The soul possesses the beloved, and exclaims, 'My beloved is mine, and I am his.' When she has grown, she does not put herself first anymore, but modestly says, 'I am my beloved's, and my beloved is mine'

(6:3). The order of the words is changed. When she has grown even more, she is satisfied in giving herself without asking for anything in return: 'I am my beloved's, and his desire is toward me' (7:10).

The Hebrew word for 'his' is *lo*, but the same word also means 'not' in spoken Hebrew (there is a difference in the way the word is written, but the oral form came first and is more significant here). The verse, when only spoken, could quite accurately be translated, 'My beloved is mine, and I am not.' He is everything in the believer's life. No place remains for a 'me.'

Those rare souls who have really attained to the truth, that the Beloved is theirs and they 'are not' anymore, have unique experiences.

By those who 'are not' I mean those who have come to the height of heights, those who in prison have known not only heavenly raptures but raptures to the *heaven of heavens* (1 Kings 8:27); those who – eluding all enquiry, withdrawn from all knowing – have come to that place from which one looks down to heaven. It is that part of the temple above of which God says, 'Behold, there is a place by me' (Exodus 33:21).

Almost all these believers died in prison or shortly after their release, like Bishop Hirtsa and Mgr Ghicay. I have had the privilege of sharing a prison cell with such a man. He did not say much. From the little he did say, I gathered that he saw what St John of the Cross and Teresa of Avila tried to describe.

He discovered that you can know things better by looking to the God in whom they have their being, life and movement than by looking at those things themselves. All things are dark. Even physical light is dark. Only he throws a light on them. Therefore the Psalmist said, 'In your light we see light' (Psalm 36:9). Others come to know God by looking at the things he has created. The mystics know the reality of creation by looking at the Creator.

Such prisoners did not see him face to face. God is

veiled, and anybody who sees God without a veil has not seen the whole reality of Godhead. The veils are part of it. If you see a man without his skin you do not see him properly, because the skin is part of who he is. It veils his inner parts, which should be veiled.

Ten doctorates and a lifetime lasting thousands of years would not teach a man what those believers saw in a single moment of such rapture.

What I have written above is an educated guess as to what they would have said, if what they knew could have been expressed in words. When they came back from this rapture, they returned as people who had seen men, events and things as God sees them. They did not say a great deal, and what they did say they said to very few. But their faces and their eyes spoke for them.

I was reminded of these, my former fellow-inmates, when I read of the manner of the conversion of Rosario Rivera, the Peruvian terrorist. She chanced to attend an evangelistic meeting led by the well-known Latin American preacher Luis Palau. Afterwards, she wrote:

> He [Luis Palau] put Rosario Rivera, who had come as an eminent member of the Peruvian Communist Party, before her own eyes in all her crude inner reality. Not even Che Guevara [her chief, and model of terrorism] could see what I was like inside, though I had been at his side for four months. But this man described my life, and brought to light the things that were deep inside me. I bit my tongue; I did not know what to do. He told me the things I had done, how I had robbed, killed, perverted young people, abused my home, trafficked in drugs, and much more besides. I saw myself stripped naked.

Luis Palau had seen her with God's eyes. But he saw her also as very beloved by God and brought her to salvation. Such is the privilege of those who 'are not'.

Mary, the mother of the Lord, is an example of how far

a human being can rise if one effaces onself before God. Jacob of Saroug, a Syrian bishop in the fifth century who composed Christian hymns, wrote in a hymn to her:

> She is highly blessed because the limits of her body have contained the Unlimited, who fills the heavens without their being able to circumscribe Him. She is most blessed, because she gave breast to the One who rules over the waves of the sea. She is most blessed, because she carried the powerful giant who carries the world. She has embraced Him and covered Him with kisses. She is most blessed, because her lips touched the One whose burning love causes angels of fire to withdraw. She is most blessed because she has nourished with her milk the One who gives life to all the world.

'My beloved is mine and I am not.' What has happened to me, when I am no more and only he remains? The aim of my life has then been fulfilled. Basil of Caesarea wrote, 'Every spiritual being is, by his nature, a temple of God created to receive in himself the glory of God.' When my Beloved is mine, and I 'am not', what is visible of me continues. But each of us has two natures: the visible and the invisible. If I have submitted to divine will, the invisible part of me has united with God.

Saint Gregory of Nyssa said that man is simultaneously a micro-cosmos and a micro-God. In the life of the bride, the micro-cosmos decreases in importance, and God, in the literal sense of the word, is magnified. Pascal wrote, 'Man is infinitely more than man.' In his own life he was able to make a reality of Jesus' words, 'You are gods' (John 10:34). When God makes his dwelling in us, we have more than mere biological, sociological and psychological possibilities within us. The sun and the moon are called 'light' in the Bible. In the same way we are called 'the light of the world.' Our possibilities are immense. Saint Gregory wrote, 'When you turn to watch him, you become what he is.' We have the aptitude for it; let us not waste it. It is for this that we were created in God's image. Let us follow the bride's passionate decision to be his. God can do everything, except compel somebody to love him. That decision must come from us.

But take care! There are beautiful compliments addressed to the people of Israel in the Bible, who were God's beloved. But, after a time, the people turned to sin, and God's opinion of them changed. We cannot simply rely on beautiful loving words addressed to us by God in the past. We must take care to abide in his love.

Feeding among lilies

The bride says, 'He feeds among the lilies' (2:6). He has said that his brides are his lilies. We, his flock, feed with him among the lilies, who already are the saints of the past and present. The example of their lives nourishes us.

A Rumanian Christian, Lydia Arsenescou, had been sentenced to death for her faith. She was a young girl of eighteen or nineteen, and she was very beautiful. Her last evening had come. The execution always took place promptly at midnight, and for this reason the Christians called the firing squad 'the midnight bride'.

Wardens had brought some gruel in pottery vessels into the cell. It was the evening meal. All the prisoners were hungry but none cared to eat. All the other women pitied the young and beautiful girl who had to die that night.

But suddenly her face began to shine. She lifted the pottery dish and said, 'I have a boyfriend. I love him greatly, and he loves me. He hoped that one day this my body would be in his embrace. But it will not be so; tonight I will be shot. And after a few years, what was my body will have become clay, just like the clay from which this pot was made. And, after a few more years, some other potter will make a vessel out of what was once my body. Who knows what is in this vessel? Perhaps what was once the beaming eye of a lover! My body will decay, but I will not die.

'Jesus said, "Whosoever lives and believes in me will never die." And I believe these words of Jesus more than the rifles which will be pointed at me tonight. I believe them more than the bullets that will pierce my chest tonight. I believe them more than the open grave which is already waiting for me.

'I am not my body. I am an eternal spirit. Tonight I shall not die. Jesus is a gentleman; he will keep his word. Tonight, by his grace, I will enter through gates of pearl into the golden city. I will see and hear angels playing on their harps. I will be with the saints and the finest men of all the centuries, and above all, I will rest on Jesus' bosom, and there I will wait for my boyfriend to come too.'

They came for her a few minutes before midnight. As she passed through the vaulted corridors of the underground prison, her voice could still be heard, reflected from wall to wall. She recited the Creed – the same Creed we all recite in church – but in her mouth, it had an entirely new significance. When she said, 'I believe in one God, maker of heaven and earth,' she really meant it. She knew; there really is a heaven. The proof was that she forsook earth for it. When she said, 'I believe in the one Lord, Jesus Christ,' the words rang true. Jesus really was her Lord. She was ready to give up her youth for him. And then they heard her last words: 'I believe in the resurrection of the body, and in life everlasting.' After this a few shots were heard. The poor Communists believed that they had killed her. They did not know that they had sent her to the embraces of the most beautiful Bridegroom of all.

On such examples, Jesus feeds us. He feeds his flock among the lilies. He has other saints as well, whose mentality is completely different to that of Christians of this century. The Church considers as saints believers such as Simon the Stylite, who remained on top of a column in the Egyptian desert for thirty years. When he was too weak to remain there, he had a post erected and chained himself to that. Many others followed his example, and stood in the burning heat of the day and the cold of the night. By doing so, they were trying to annihilate the part of them that lusted after sin.

Saint Etheldreda also believed that the flesh is evil and dirty. She refused to cleanse it, and walked about unwashed. So did the man whom Church history records as St Anthony the Great, who is remembered for his stand with St Athanasius in the great fight against the Arian heresy.

We would not enjoy being in the company of such people. But when a reed is bent, the only way to straighten it is to bend it in the opposite direction. In a world in which so many die from hunger and others spend their money on useless creams and costly perfumes, it is good that here and there individuals exist who demonstrate, by extreme attitudes, the vanity of our way of life. They too are lilies, among whom Jesus feeds his flock.

Christians were prevented from washing for weeks, months and sometimes years in Communist prisons, and they became full of lice, loathsome to themselves and others. It was a very great help to them, and a reinforcement of their faith, to remember that there were once saints who adopted this burden voluntarily.

Jesus feeds his sheep among lilies. No other shepherd can do that.

The sending away of the Beloved

The bride says, 'Until the day break, and the shadows flee away, turn, my beloved, and be like a roe or a young hart upon the mountins of Bether' (2:17). I know of a Christian who was in solitary confinement for years, in much hunger and pain. Sometimes he was aware of Jesus asking him, 'Is it too difficult for you? Shall I ease your lot?' Again and again he replied, 'Please, Jesus, see to others. I can bear it; I'm all right.'

This is the mentality of the bride. She tells Jesus to follow his calling as a king. She can carry the cross allotted to her in the hope that, when the evening comes, he will return to her. She is reluctant to make continual demands upon him.

When the apostle Peter realized who Jesus was, he said to him, 'Depart from me; for I am a sinful man' (Luke 5:8). Peter was very grateful that Jesus had increased his catch to an exceptionally great multitude of fish. But he also knew that a being like Jesus could do greater things than merely provide a fisherman with a miraculous haul. Like the bride in the Song, he wanted him to go away and do his more marvellous work. Peter was prepared to be content with a normal-sized catch.

The bride sends the Bridegroom away to the mountains of Bether (2:17). The word *bether* means 'separation'. She believes it is possible to exist without him, to be separate from him. This thought brings us to the third chapter of the Song of Songs, a book so important that Origen, one of the distinguished teachers of the Church in the third century, wrote twelve volumes about it. Saint Bernard of Clairvaux delivered eighty-six sermons on the first two chapters alone. The great German writer, Goethe, called it 'the most divine of all love songs.' Herder said of it, 'The song is written as though from paradise.' It is a book which repays thorough study.

≈ *Chapter 3* ≈

Seeking the Bridegroom

The bride says: 'By night on my bed I sought him whom my soul loves: I sought him, but I found him not. I will rise now, and go about the city in the streets, and in the broad ways I will seek him whom my soul loves: I sought him, but I found him not' (3:1–2). Theologians will tell you, 'It is difficult to find God; wherewith will you find him?' Dionysius the Areopagite wrote:

> If it should happen that somebody should see God and understand what he sees, then he has not seen God Himself . . . for He surpasses any intelligence and any essence. He exists only to the degree to which He is totally unknown . . .
>
> Thus we say that the Universal Cause situated beyond the whole universe is neither matter nor body.
>
> It has no face. It has no shape, no form, no quality, no mass. It is in no place, it cannot be apprehended by our senses . . . Ascending higher, we say now that this Cause has no soul and no intelligence . . . It cannot be expressed, nor conceived.
>
> It has no number, no order, no grandeur, no smallness, no equality, no similitude, no dissimilitude. It does not rest unmoved; neither does it move. It is neither power nor light. It does not live and is not life.
>
> It is not essence, nor perpetuity, nor time. It has no knowledge, no truth, no wisdom. It is not one, nor

unity, nor divinity, nor good; neither spirit nor affiliation nor paternity, in the sense we use this word.

But the bride mistrusts philosophy – even religious philosophy. She seeks him diligently, night after night (the Hebrew word in verse 1 means 'nights'). She has been promised that, provided she does not seek the living among the dead, she will not seek in vain: 'Whoever seeks, shall find' (Luke 11:10). She deceived herself when she imagined she could live separated from him; now she seeks him.

You cannot find him from a bed of ease, lying quietly in comfort. You have to strive. The bride realizes that her sighing, and demanding and others' intervention do not bring her the Beloved. The soul must become active; it must practise spiritual exercises.

Exposing herself to all the risks which any girl runs who walks alone at night-time, the bride walks on darkened streets, seeking her Beloved. She travels all kinds of roads. There is no place where she does not seek him. She looks in the face of every passer-by, to see if she can can glean information from anybody about the one she loves.

But the Beloved is not a man of public places. Righteous men usually shun such places, because there one can expect to find mostly evil. Jesus too lived, for the most part, a private life. When He was twelve years old, his parents lost him. They looked for him in the wrong place; in the caravan, where he never is. So he asked them, when they found him, 'How is it that you sought me?' He told them where he always is, where he can readily be found by anybody: at 'My Father's business' (Luke 2:49). That is the only place where he may legitimately be sought.

Jesus said these words not only to Mary, but also to his adoptive father, Joseph. What we must understand from this is that the child had already made up his mind. His supreme ambition was not to be an assistant in Joseph's workshop. He had another Father, a heavenly Father; and he was going to be in his service.

The watchmen of the city

The bride says, 'The watchmen that go about the city found me: to whom I said, "Saw you him whom my soul loves?" It was but a little that I passed from them, but I found him whom my soul loves: I held him, and would not let him go, until I had brought him into my mother's house, and into the chamber of her that conceived me' (3:3–4). The watchmen of the city are the bishops, priests, pastors, preachers, rabbis and mullahs of different religions. Some brides fall in love with them and with their ornate services and beautiful sermons, and because of these they forget to go on seeking the Bridegroom himself, whom you can find only when you go on from them. You find Jesus only when you have left every creature behind.

In practice it is difficult to distinguish the ambitions of such as Horeb, Datan and Abiram (who in the Old Testament rebelled against Moses, the God-appointed authority over the people) from those of the brides who, because of their unlimited love for Jesus, leave the watchmen behind without despising them. But it is not for us to judge others. We trust that everyone does the best of which he is capable.

In the end, the bride finds the Beloved outside the city, at night. And what energy she shows then! She takes hold of him, and says to him – as Jacob once said to an angel – 'I will not leave you until you bless me.' She took hold of him and would not let him go. Simply to find Jesus, is not enough. You must also know how to keep him.

The bride brings him into the house of her mother, the Church. Saint Cyprian said, 'Whosoever has God as his Father, has the Church as his mother.' The worth of a church service consists only in the fact that the worshippers, the brides, have come to the service bringing Jesus with them.

There are some very bad church leaders. Many

Protestant and Catholic church leaders have remained silent about the closure of tens of thousands of churches in Russia, China North Korea and Albania. Even worse than that, some Catholic and Protestant church leaders praise the persecuters, describing them as nice people. Other church leaders, while probably being worthy individuals, are not truly ready to die for what they believe.

In the Rumanian prison of Piteshti, prisoners were forced to actively deny their faith by gross blasphemy of the Eucharist. They were made to scream sacred melodies, in which filthy words replaced those of the hymns. They were made to gesture degradingly with their genitals. They were made to eat excrement. This obscene parody of the Eucharist was intended to transform the worship into a demonic drama of evil and hatred.

The result was minds in chaos. The brainwashers thereby achieved mastery of the prisoners, who identified with their new masters and so felt loyalty to them. Then the prisoners were expected to prove that loyalty by inflicting torment on another group of inmates. Should one of these 're-educated' prisoners be observed to be lenient in his beating of others or careless in depriving them of sleep, such mercy was interpreted as a breach of his new loyalty. He would then be put through the agony again himself.

Sometimes Christians who, after unspeakable tortures, had turned Communist in prison were asked to conceal their new loyalty. They invented a so-called fake Christian organisation and enlisted teenage prisoners. Those teenagers believed that they had found 'watchmen' who could tell them about the Bridegroom. Imagine the shock in the hearts of those young people when the very teachers who had brought them to Christ at a pre-arranged signal produced cudgels and beat them viciously. They were assaulted until they denied Christ, whose adoration their persecuters had previously taught.[1]

In Guyana, 'Reverend' Jim Jones, leader of the People's Temple, ordered the suicide of all his followers and the slaughter of their children. In all 920 people died. Jones was a 'watchman' who had mixed Marxism with Christianity, a mixture in which the latter always perishes, leaving only murders and Marxism.

Horrors such as this and the atrocities at Piteshti were happening at a time when Communism was well spoken of by some church leaders in the East and the West. Obviously, a bride has to leave such 'watchmen' behind, if she is to find Christ himself.

But there are also some very trustworthy church leaders. The late Rumanian Bishop Hossu, who spent twenty-two years in prison, said, 'You cannot know how painful the suffering of a bishop is, over the sad destiny of his church and his nation. It can only be compared to the torment of Jesus in Gethsemane and on the cross, when He foresaw all the persecutions that would be unleashed through the centuries, by the enemies of the church.' Another trustworthy leader was the Russian Adventist Shtshelkov, who died in prison aged eighty-four, after twenty-four years in jail, standing firm for what he believed. Sadly, such leaders are few and far between.

But the bride does not need to stop at pastors. We are not limited to hearing the Word only from them. The bride in Solomon's Song finds Jesus when she leaves the watchmen behind. She finds sweetness even in barbed wire thorns. In Siberian snows, among ferocious prison guards, brides of Christ detect the fragrance of the Rose of Sharon and the Lily of the Valleys in the smells, sights and sounds of the concentration camps.

In Golgothaean Christianity, personal meetings with Jesus are frequently described. Saint Bernard of Clairvaux wrote:

I never knew the precise moment of the coming of the Word. I felt His presence. I remember He was with me.

I sometimes had a presentiment that He would come, but I sensed neither His coming nor His going. I do not know where He went after leaving me, nor by what means He came and went.

You will ask me how I know that He was present, if His coming was incomprehensible. I will reply that He is alive and full of energy. Immediately upon entering me, He awoke my sleeping soul. He aroused and softened and taught my heart, which had been as hard as stone. He began uprooting and pulling down, planting and building, watering the dry places and lightening the dark ones.

There have been some visions of angels and of Christ in the prisons, but these are not the norm. More often one can tell that the bride has seized hold of Christ by the profound change in the attitude of the Christian prisoners.

The beautiful daughter of the Lutheran pastor, Traube, worked in the office of a Soviet Collective. The local Communist Party secretary offered her the choice of becoming his lover or seeing her father arrested and his church closed. After a long resistance she yielded. She became pregnant, hanged herself, and left a letter in her pocket explaining why she had done so.

A comrade found the letter and brought it to the guilty Communist, who destroyed it and forged another in her handwriting. It claimed that her father had raped her and that she could not bear the shame. As a result the father was sentenced and the church was closed.

Sex offenders in jail are attacked by other prisoners. Though falsely accused, Pastor Traube suffered a great deal at the hands of his fellow-inmates. He tried to pray, in vain. He could not say the words, 'Forgive them Father, for they know not what they do.' He could not forgive the wicked wrong done to him by the Communists. He became ill.

One day, a new prisoner was put in the cell. It was the

man responsible for his daughter's death, the closure of his church and all the torment he had undergone. The Communist had been jailed for embezzlement.

When Traube realized the misery that this criminal was experiencing – overburdened by guilt, jailed by his own comrades, lacking any knowledge of the Saviour – he drowned his own sufferings in the much deeper ones of the Communist. On his deathbed, the pastor finally said the Lord's Prayer right through. He forgave. He died with a look of radiance on his face. He had the soul of a bride who has sought the Beloved, and at the end had seized hold of him. He had had a personal meeting with Jesus.

Christ, known in personal experiences in exceptional circumstances such as these, can be brought to the mother's house, the Church. The Church will be greatly blessed by our encounters with Christ.

The bride ascends from the desert

The bride says, 'Who is this that comes out of the wilderness like pillars of smoke, perfumed with myrrh and frankincense, with all the powders of the merchant? Behold his [palanquin], which is Solomon's' (3:6–7). The bride has passed out of the city into the desert, and she has learned a great deal there. The desert is not in fact as arid as people believe. Thousands of different plants thrive there. What characterizes them all is great adaptability. Without it, in a region with little rain and a summer temperature above 120 degrees, they would be lost. The bride could not survive either, were she not adaptable to different social structures and political regimes.

The saguaro is a cactus of the Arizona desert. Its roots, seeking out every drop of moisture, can spread as far as a hundred feet. During rainfall it takes in reserves of water like a camel, in preparation for dry periods which can last for years. It literally grows fat with water. Its girth can increase by half, or even more. One saguaro was found to contain more than thirty tons of liquid, 'an engineering feat which probably has no parallel in any artificial structure in existence.' Similarly, in the spiritual desert the bride learns to be deeply rooted in the Kingdom and to provide herself abundantly with the water of life.

When she was seven, my daughter Amely was not much of an eater. She only wanted to eat desserts. Once I chided her about this. She said to me, 'I eat as it says in the Bible! It says there that God wants us to live on desserts only.' She showed me the verse: 'God led his people forty years through the desert.' She was not wholly wrong. Life in the desert is a delicacy, a dessert reserved for God's beloved.

What a marvellous sight it must have been when the people of Israel came from the desert to the country of Canaan, or when they returned to their own country from the Babylonian captivity. It is the same when a soul returns to God from the desert of this world and cleaves to Jesus. Thereby it enters into a state of grace, and the bride is brought to the Bridegroom.

Should we be frugal in anointing Jesus with myrrh? It was Judas Iscariot who criticized the woman who anointed Jesus before his arrest.

The valiant men

The bride says, 'Threescore valiant men are about [Solomon's bed], of the valiant of Israel. They all hold swords, being expert in war: every man has his sword upon his thigh because of fear in the night' (3:7–8). The Church has never lacked valiant men. On 15 August 1714, the Rumanian king Constantin Brincoveanu died a martyr death. For the twenty-five years of his reign he had been a valiant defender of the Christian world against Islam. On Good Friday 1714 he and his whole household were arrested by the Turkish sultan's men and taken to Constantinople, where they were put in the notorious Yedikuleh prison. On his sixtieth birthday, Brincoveanu was sentenced to death together with his four sons.

Before the executioner raised his axe, the sultan said, 'I will pardon you, if you tell me where the wealth of your country is, and if you will deny the Christian faith and convert to Islam.'

Brincoveanu replied, 'I will never abandon the Christian faith. I was born in it, have lived in it and will die in it. I have filled my country with churches, monasteries and hospitals. I will not worship in your mosques, neither I nor my children.' Then he turned to his sons. 'My beloved, be strong in faith. We have lost all things. Let us not lose our souls as well.'

The sultan ordered that the sons should die first. Young Constantin prayed and quietly put his head on the block. As he was beheaded, his father sighed. 'God, your will be done.' The next two sons followed. Then Matthew, who was only sixteen, wavered at the sight of the blood and hid himself near his mother. 'Follow your brothers,' urged Brincovaneau. 'Do not deny Christ.' The youngster put his head on the block and said to the executioner, 'Strike'.

The king followed them. Kneeling, he prayed with many tears. 'God, accept our sacrifice. For the blood of our martyrdom, I desire that the Rumanian principates should remain Christian. Amen.'

In the seventeenth century, in what is now Massachusetts, a law was passed declaring that all Quakers entering the British colony should be whipped, imprisoned and put to forced labour. Every exiled Quaker who returned was to be hanged. The 'crime' of the Quakers was their belief in an inner illumination, a direct communion with God without the intermediary of clergy or ritual.

Mary Dyer, though she had been whipped and threatened with death, came again and again to the colony from Rhode Island to visit her brethren in jail. Finally Mary and two others were sentenced to hang. She attended the execution of the other two, then her hands were tied and a black sack was put over her head. But at the last moment she was reprieved and deported.

She returned again. She was risking public flagellation, and having her tongue pierced with a red hot iron. At her trial she declared, 'If you do not revoke your unjust laws, the Lord will send other witnesses of the truth after my death. Compared with liberty and truth, my life does not matter.' For this she died, valiant Christian. There is a statue honouring her in Boston.

Nowadays, Christians who would behave towards imprisoned believers in Communist prisons as she did towards the suffering brethren of that time are rare. God has valiant men and women, but they are few.

William Booth, a Hebrew Christian, founded the Salvation Army. His followers called him 'General', which made him a laughing stock. His motto was, 'Go for souls and go for the worst.' Today he would have said, 'Go for Communist torturers and murderers.'

He went about with men he called 'godly daredevils', a mob of uneducated but converted men chosen from saloons, brothels and gambling houses. The owners of such places counterattacked. Salvation Army preachers were drenched with the contents of chamberpots. Booth did not care. He ordered his Army to charge into saloons and drag drunkards out for conversion.

Today the Army is active in 92 countries. It preaches in 111 languages and operates 900 schools in non-Christian lands. In many countries it has influenced social legislation. Booth was another valiant man around Solomon's bed. Even today we have such valiant men.

Some of the special tortures devised by Communists for Christians are described by the Rumanian Communist writer Paul Goma. One prisoner was 'baptized' daily by having his head stuck in the barrel which served as a communal lavatory, while other prisoners were made to sing the baptismal service.

During festivals, and especially Lent, blasphemous masses were organised. One prisoner was dressed in an excrement-smeared robe. Round his neck, in place of the cross, was hung a phallus made of a mixture of bread, soap and DDT. All the prisoners were forced to kiss it and pronounce the sacred Orthodox formula, 'Christ is resurrected.'

What do these indignities have to do with Socialism and the interests of the proletariat? They are nothing more than satanic orgies. Some valiant Christians refused to participate, and as a consequence they died under torture.

When Christians have to bear crosses they make roses blossom in them. The life and death of the Lutheran pastor Joseph Jurash of Czechoslovakia will illustrate what I mean. He had been invited to become a collaborator, but had refused. So the Communists sentenced him to thirteen years of imprisonment. They inserted sharp objects under his fingernails and toenails and pierced his body with needles. Soon after his release from prison he died. A fellow prisoner wrote of him, 'His personality glowed in a special way.'[5]

In the Soviet Union, over a hundred people gathered in a single room at the house of Brother Kozorezov when he returned from prison. He preached to them from Matthew 5:10: 'Blessed are they which are persecuted for righteousness' sake, for theirs is the kingdom of heaven'. Flowers were presented to him. A nun named Sister Alia spoke of her recent arrest, and the surprise of the Secret Police officer when she told him she had to pray first before answering his questions. She knelt in his presence and did the same when the interrogation was over. A major watching was impressed and helped her to rise from her knees. (All our discussions would be more peaceful if we practised the same habit in our daily lives. In Korea I have seen brethren praying first when they entered one another's houses, and only then conversing.)

A tape of this meeting in the USSR was sent to us. On it, police can be heard shouting, 'Finish! Disperse! To hell with you!'

Kozorezov can be heard answering, 'We preach the love of Christ.'

A police officer: 'What do I care? It's forbidden here. Disperse while we're still speaking politely to you.'

Kozorezov replies. 'We are servants of love. Whence comes the evil?'

The police officer retorts, 'I know nothing of that. I want no sermons. You are not allowed to gather here.'

As the tape finishes, the choir begins to sing.

Such as these are today's valiant men around the Bridegroom's bed. In the Hebrew it says of them, 'They are held by the sword.' It will not let them go. They are the slaves of the sword of the Spirit, which is the Word of God.

Solomon's palanquin

The bride says, 'King Solomon made himself a chariot [= palanquin] of the wood of Lebanon. He made the pillars thereof of silver, the bottom thereof of gold, the covering of it of purple, the midst thereof being paved with love, for the daughters of Jerusalem' (3:9–10). There are still many things that are wrong in the bride's heart, but she is in Solomon's palanquin the pillars of which are of silver. In the Bible the Word of God is described as silver cleansed in the furnace. So the palanquin is based on God's Word. The covering is of purple, which means that the bride is covered by the blood of Jesus, shed for her.

The interior of the palanquin is paved with love shown by the daughters of Zion. Love is belittled in our world, as mere sentimentalism or time-wasting. In reality it works very efficiently. Mary Magdalene, when sitting at Jesus' feet, seemed to be doing nothing. In fact, she was doing the most important thing of all – she was loving. While she appeared to be quietly sitting, her love was weaving beautiful ornaments for Solomon's bed, in which she herself would later rest. It is not our service that Jesus seeks, but our love. Only a faith that engenders love has value in his eyes.

There is a love that forgives all things. In his book, *It Was Not the Black Cat*, the former Rumanian Zionist prisoner T. Lavi describes how prisoners were mockingly called 'parrots', and were forced to spend hours shouting brief sentences deriding their creed. They could either repeat, 'Jesus is not the Son of God' or utter obscenities about the Virgin. Jewish prisoners likewise were forced to say ugly things about their religion. Before having to declaim their blasphemous sentences, they had to run for whole nights around their cells, being whipped if they ran too slowly. The Hungarian Cardinal Mindszenty was one who endured such treatment. The alternative to uttering blasphemy was to face being beaten to a pulp.

Many were weak. Nobody should be taken in by the notion that all who are in prison for their faith are men of heroism, full of virtues and endurance. It is not so. Many Christians who suffered there were frail. Many gave in and said words that no Christian ought to pronounce. And then followed the self-justifications: 'After all, I am only a man!' . . . 'What does it matter if I say these things? God does not worry about it' . . . 'Surely God would rather I live, than die for refusing to say a few words – anyway, the words are nonsense.'

Some went to the other extreme. In their consciences

they heard not voices of self-justification, but accusations which drove them to despair. In Red China, many who had denied Christ, or betrayed secrets of the Underground Church under torture, hanged themselves or threw themselves out of windows.

The true bride of Christ does not need to go to either extreme. The Word of God gives her comfort and teaches her about forgiveness. Even when her fall has been a heavy one, she knows she can rest in the palanquin of Solomon. We who are free, and have sinned greatly, can do so as well.

The mother's merit

The bride says, 'Go forth, O daughters of Zion, and behold King Solomon with the crown wherewith his mother crowned him in the day of his espousals, and in the day of the gladness of his heart' (3:11). In this passage Solomon, the wise and rich king – the builder of the Temple of God – is a type of the Saviour Jesus, for whom the name of Solomon is also fitting. In Hebrew it means 'peace'. The mother of Solomon is a type of Jesus' mother. There is still a custom in the Oriental Orthodox Church that the bridegroom's mother puts a crown on his head.

Christ has possessed glorious crowns from all eternity – the crown of the eternal Sonship of God, the crown of love, of goodness, and of wisdom – but he owes one crown to his mother. She gave him something that he had never had before: a human nature. She made him man as well as God. It was her gift to him, at the wedding of the godly and the human that was his conception. God had always known the life of all men, but from the outside, so to speak; from the perspective of Godhead. Now he knew it from the inside.

Under the Communist regimes, many former judges and prosecutors in the old capitalist system were jailed. Having now experienced prison for themselves they regretted the harsh sentences they had passed earlier. A few years of prison may not sound very much in the mouth of the judge, they realized, but those same few years of jail meant great suffering to the sentenced prisoner. 'Every minute spent in prison is a bitter pill like no other,' one judge said. 'Had I known this, I would have been less harsh in my judgements.'

Because of the obedience of Mary, by whom he became man, God was able to experience human life and know it from the inside. He was tempted in all things, just like us. He experienced the inner struggles we experience, and because of this, we have in him a merciful and faithful High Priest (Hebrews 2:17). That is why all nations call Mary 'blessed'.

Onute Vitkauskaite, a Lithuanian Christian prisoner, wrote this letter to her mother on Mother's Day:

> There is so much to think about and remember. But let's leave all that in the care of our beloved mother Mary. She taught our mothers love, sacrifice and kindness. May the humiliation and scorn that we suffer be as a prayer of thanksgiving for that! But I would also like it to be a form of atonement for those so-called mothers, who, without the least twinge of conscience, murder not only the bodies but also the souls of infants. Having scorned the Mother of Love, they have lost the source from which they could draw love, kindness and strength on the road of maternal sacrifice. In the labour camp I have come to discover how terrible is man's life without God, without eternal love.

Another Lithuanian prisoner, Julius Sasnaukas, wrote to his family on the same Mother's Day:

> My best wishes to Mother and Grandmother. It is

difficult to find the right words for this occasion. Here by my bunk I have a tiny Leonardo Madonna on a postage stamp and it seems that life, love and eternal spring seep into this dismal abode.

It can help us all to think frequently of the beautiful example of the virgin Mary.

≈ Chapter 4 ≈

The bride with no veil

The Bridegroom says:

> Behold, you are fair, my love; you are fair; you have doves' eyes within your locks: your hair is as a flock of goats, that appear from Mount Gilead.
> Your teeth are like a flock of sheep that are even shorn, which came up from the washing; whereof every one bears twins, and none is barren among them.
> Your lips are like a thread of scarlet, and your speech is comely; your temples are like a piece of pomegranate within your locks.
> Your neck is like the tower of David built for an armoury, whereon hang a thousand bucklers, all shields of mighty men.
> Your two breasts are like two young roes that are twins, which feed among the lilies.
>
> (4:1-5)

In those days (and even today in some Moslem countries), girls in the Orient walked with their faces veiled. The bridegroom sees the bride unveiled for the first time only after the wedding ceremony. Then he sees the beauties which were hidden from him until that moment. When our Bridegroom comes, we will be like him, and he will discover in us unspeakable splendours; and we will give them to him, to give him pleasure.

The greatest beauties, in the case of this bride, are her 'doves' eyes'. Like those of God, they are so clean that they cannot even see evil, and cannot look upon unrighteousness. The two rows of her teeth represent her faith and meditation, by which the soul feeds upon Jesus. They are white as shorn sheep when they come up from the washing. Her faith is white and pure, not faked.

Her teeth are strong; strength is a characteristic of this bride. The teeth are covered by lips – usually they are not seen. So, the bride has a hidden faith in her clean conscience, not a self-advertising faith which shouts in the marketplaces. And, just as the teeth chew the food for the whole body, not for themselves, the souls of brides spend themselves in the service of others, keeping back nothing for themselves. Each sheep bears twins. Christians, like twins, share identical attitudes, because they are of one heart and of one soul.

Her lips are like a thread of scarlet. That shows that she is healthy. Her temples are like half a pomegranate, a fruit with red seeds which are easily seen when it is cut. This reminds us of a pure girl, blushing in humility at the remembrance of her sin and unworthiness. This modesty makes the bride attractive in the Bridegroom's eyes.

The neck is what joins the body to the head. The Church is the body; Jesus its head. What unites them is faith. The faith of the bride is strong, therefore, the Bridegroom tells her, 'Your neck is like the tower of David built for an armoury.' In antiquity, towers were adorned with shields or bucklers. So the tower of David – representing the faith of the bride – has a thousand shields hanging on it, all shields of mighty men. They are reminders of the battles of the saints of old, who have defeated the devil, the world and sinful nature.

The way the name 'David' is written here is unusual. When it first appears in the Bible, 'David' is written *DVD*. When David commits great sins, as when he took the wife of one of his soldiers, it is written like that. But David had beautiful moments in his life as well. At such times a *Y*, the first letter of God's name, is added, and it is written *DVYD*. That is how his name is written at the end of his life's story. He had his wanderings, but he finished the course well. And now, in the Hebrew text of the Song, David's name is not only written *DVYD*, to emphasise the godly side of his character, but above it is inscribed a circle, showing that because his son has written a song such as this, David has reached the highest point of union with God.

The breasts of the bride look like a meadow full of lilies on which two young roes graze. Souls who have wept for Jerusalem will drink the milk of its comforts.

The mountain of myrrh

The bride, having heard so many words of comfort from the Bridegroom, makes him this promise:
'Until the day break, and the shadows flee away, I will get me to the mountain of myrrh, and to the hill of frankincense' (4:6). There she will stay until the miseries of this life pass away.

The mountain of myrrh recalls Mount Moriah, on which the Temple was built, and in which so much incense mixed with spices was burnt daily to the glory of God that (so says the *Talmud*) the daughters of Jerusalem did not need to perfume themselves. There the bride will retire for prayer.

We can be sure that our Lord, as he sees the brides who suffer for him today in Communist and Islamic prisons, has the same words of admiration and wonder for them as he has for the bride of Solomon's Song.

The Lithuanian Christian prisoner, Mrs Ona Pranskunaite, describes in a letter how she was transported from prison to labour camp in a railway wagon divided into tiny cells. From a nearby cell, the Christian Lapienis comforted her with words from Scripture, and from Thomas à Kempis' *The Imitation of Christ*: He said, 'Onute, let us try to fulfil our assignment from God, so as to serve his glory in the honour of our nation.' Ona wrote:

> I will march with strength, eyes toward heaven, wherever the torments of life lead me. Everyone has a treasure worthy of being protected. Trusting in the grace of the Lord and in your prayers, I am sure to find the strength to bear all difficulties. I fear only one thing – that I might do evil.
>
> Do not worry about me. I find comfort and joy in prayer, in sacrifice, and in trying to help my comrades in suffering. Here we work fourteen to fifteen hours a day.
>
> Brethren and sisters in Christ, do not fear the tempests of our times. God permits suffering but also gives us strength to bear it. The believers who sold their consciences for a plate of lentils, and became our persecutors, need penitence. So do we.

Cardinal Mindszenty of Hungary wrote from his insect-ridden cell, 'We are small; but we can grow. The saints always reached heights when they descended into the most profound depths of human suffering. Lord, grant me only a morsel of the strength of saints.' During the civil war following their revolution, Russian Communists tortured the Orthodox priest George Snesarev of Voronesh. Nails were driven under his fingernails and toenails. He was wounded sixty-three times. Seven nuns of the Protection Convent were boiled in a cauldron of tar. Their crime? They had been praying for anti-Communists. The monk, Nektary Ivanov, was made to drink 'communion wine' made with molten pewter.[1]

In all such atrocities many Christians remained faithful to their Bridegroom. Their deeds and their beauty are outstanding, like the breasts of the bride.

All fair

The Bridegroom says, 'You are all fair, my love; there is no spot in you. Look from the top of Amana, from the top of Shenir and Hermon, from the lions' dens, from the mountains of the leopards' (4:7-8). The decision of the bride to give herself to prayer makes her even more attractive in the Bridegroom's eyes. He calls her 'all fair . . . without a spot.' (This is, incidentally, a good example of how husbands should regard their wives. The apostle Paul says, 'Husbands, love your wives, even as Christ also loved the church, and gave himself for it' (Ephesians 5:25). He, loving his Church, saw her to be all fair and without a spot. We must have doves' eyes like him.)

He calls her 'bride' for the first time. How did she come to bear the proud title of the bride of God's Son? It is because she gave herself for him in persecution, just as he gave himself for her.

A Rumanian Christian named Babutz had much to tell when he arrived in America. He told how prisoners were systematically beaten on the kidneys, after sandbags had been placed on their bodies to prevent marks.

Together with thousands of others he had been sent to a slave labour camp. His job was to clean the weeds from the River Danube, by hand. Many prisoners, standing waist-deep in the icy water in winter, died. Coming and going, the prisoners had to look at the swollen corpses of their friends exhibited at the entrance to the camp. They were told, 'That will be your fate as well, if you do not meet your quota.'

In winter, their thick clothing was taken from them. They were told, 'The cold will make you work harder.' Prisoners went hungry when the rats ate what little they received. One hid a slice of bread in his shirt, saving it for the next day. In the night mice chewed through his shirt and ate the bread.

Another, forced to work in the fields, stole 20 onions to

share with his friends. He was caught. He was made to choose between eating them all at once or getting twenty-five lashes on the soles of his feet. To avoid the excruciating pain of the flogging he began to eat the onions. Soon he collapsed, his eyes swollen from their sockets, like a frog's eyes.

Yet another caught a serpent and tried to roast it on the guards' fire. When caught he was made to eat the serpent raw. Once an almost blind prisoner came to Babutz joyously, wanting to share with him some crumbs of maize cake he had found. Babutz told him, 'It is not maize cake. It is mouse droppings.' The other exclaimed, 'Get away with your dirty jokes!' and ate the droppings. For months they were given no salt with their food. Then suddenly it was saturated with salt. Many fell sick.

Babutz's daughter was told that she could only be accepted for college if she denounced her father for 'compelling her to be a believer', a charge which would mean he would be sentenced again.

But if you want to see happy people, you should look at men like Babutz, and the others who have suffered in Rumanian jails. They have taken a course in happiness; they drown their sorrows in the deep ocean of Jesus' tears for the sins of the world and the sufferings of his flock. Their own pain counts little beside his.

Let us try to do the same. We may be degraded. We may be frustrated. But we surely never ate mouse droppings. Let us take up our crosses joyfully. Then we too will hear the words of the Bridegroom, 'Come with me from Lebanon, my spouse; come from the lions' dens.'

Come from Lebanon

Lebanon is a range of mountains separating Syria, a

heathen country, from the Holy Land. We have left heathendom; but we have not yet arrived in the Promised Land. We are still in the Lebanese mountains, 'the mountains of leopards,' full of savage beasts. But from the mountains of Lebanon one can see Israel, the heavenly fatherland, where we will be with the Most Beloved. Even the mountains over which we must pass are full of beauty.

'Look from the top of Amana' says the Bridegroom. It is from here that the rivers Amana and Parpar flow – rivers of which Naaman the Syrian spoke when he said, 'Their waters are better than all the waters of Israel.' On top of Mount Amana, we are not yet in the Promised Land, but here we experience joys, some of which we shall not even know in heaven. It is a joy to win souls for the heavenly kingdom. That joy we can only know on earth – and how intense a joy it is!

Only here can we know the joy of faith. In heaven there will be no faith, only sight. There are other joys awaiting us, but we will be deprived of the joy of faith. We who for the present know only these joys, value them. And we also are tempted to say that the rivers which flow from Amana are better than all the waters of Israel.

'Look . . . from the top of Shenir'. The *Targum of Jerusalem*, an ancient Aramaic translation of the Bible, says that on this mountain so much fruit grows that it cannot all be harvested, and much of it rots. Here the bride learns to bring her fullness of harvest to the Bridegroom.

It is interesting to observe that the 'lions' dens', the dens of those lions which desire to consume believers, are situated on the heights of Amana. *Amana* shares the same root as the Hebrew word for 'faith', *Emunah*. Nowhere is one exposed to the devil's attacks so much as on these peaks. Where you bring most fruit, you attract his worst fury.

Those who have not themselves passed through the lions' dens, who have always lived in comfortable places and never on the mountains of leopards, who do not ascend the peaks of faith and prayer, are often apathetic towards the sufferings of their brothers and sisters in Christ.

In the Soviet Union the Orthodox priest Yakunin sheltered Christians of every denomination for fifteen years. When he was arrested, I received a smuggled letter from another Orthodox in Russia, describing these past activities of Yakunin the priest. He said they were convinced that the authorities would never touch him; Yakunin was well known, and so they would be afraid of the uproar his imprisonment would arouse in the West. However, the letter continued:

> No vociferous complaints, no mass demonstrations followed his arrest. No voice which could have awakened the western public was raised in time.
>
> It seems that even the Soviet authorites were surprised that the arrest of a well known priest and defender of religious freedom should arouse such a minimal reaction in the West. Because they now knew there would be no protest, very soon afterwards the Communists arrested the renowned Hebrew Christian historian, Regelson; and then came the Soviet attack upon Afghanistan.
>
> Afterwards another witness for Christ, the priest Dudko, ascended the Golgotha prepared for him a long time ago. [Dudko and Regelson later recanted under duress.] The Adventist leader, Shtshelkov, who suffered greatly for his Christian faith, died at the age of eighty-four in Yakutia prison camp.
>
> So it will continue if we remain silent and forget the sufferers. We must appeal to men of good will throughout the entire world. I have no words to express my despair and my feelings of powerlessness.

One is reminded of this passage in Isaiah:

'None calls for justice, nor any pleads for truth . . . [The Lord] saw that there was no man, and wondered that there was no intercessor' (59:4, 16).

But those who have been in the lions' den provide examples of spiritual beauty. A prisoner in Cuba wrote to his wife, 'The Holy Spirit brings your love and prayers to me daily. Even if I don't receive your letters, angels keep us a united, happy and contented family which rests in the arms of the King, Jesus.' This should be a lesson to those who have their marriage partners close to them and yet have not learned happiness.

In Communist countries there is not only a dreadful oppression, but also a Christian resistance to it. When you read of it, your spirit rejoices. There are heroes in our time. When one lives in tragic circumstances miracles become everyday events. 'He who has not suffered has not seen God. We will not see Him from satellites, but in the lives of those who are not afraid of suffering.' So wrote Dudko before his arrest and downfall. Others who suffered even more under the Communists did not crack.

The Soviet professor, Tatiana Shtshipkova, wrote,

I refused even to talk to the officials of the secret police. To talk to them is the first step towards collaboration. I was driven from my job as teacher of Roman history at the university, because I spoke of my faith. I showed the Bible to students who had never seen one before. My son and his girlfriend were expelled from the Institute also.

My daughter Liuba, a non-believer, was expelled from the Communist youth organization because she had not denounced me as a Christian. After this, Liuba became a believer.

A group of policemen behaved in an unseemly way towards us. I slapped one of them. I expect a one-year sentence for this.

Ogorodnikov is sentenced for one year. He has turned from Marxism to a deep Christian faith.

Ermolaev, nineteen years old, is imprisoned because in the subway he expressed his opinion about the Communist Party.

We have no aggressive intentions. We cause no upheavals, we print no leaflets, we do not preach insurrection. We wish to live as Christ taught, which means, we want to live and pray together, help each other, witness to our faith and speak of Christ to those who want to listen. Are we dangerous? Surely so; the proof lies with the persecutors.

The well-deserved slap which Shtshipkova gave the policeman for his obscene gesture reminds us of Archbishop Luke of Tashkent. He shook the ladders on which the Communist workmen were climbing in order to tear down the crosses from the cupola of his cathedral. Then, because he was also a doctor, he took care of their bruises.

Many Christians have given their lives for Christ. Six Soviet Baptists who were sent to Afghanistan as soldiers were executed there, because they refused to shoot Afghan freedom fighters. They righly judged that the Soviet Army had no business to be in a peaceful neighbouring country. It is right to defend a free fatherland, but it is wrong to fight in the name of a God-hating, murderous regime. They came from Lebanon, from the lions' dens, from the mountains of leopards, and are now in the embrace of Jesus.

They knew the biblical way of happiness: 'You have loved righteousness, and hated iniquity; therefore God, even your God, has anointed you with gladness above your fellows' (Hebrews 1:9). They loved the righteous commandment, 'Do not kill.' They hated the iniquity of Soviet rule and died for their convictions. Now they know the unsurpassed happiness of heaven. In addition, they experienced hours of jubilation before their execution, just as Jesus went singing toward Gethsemane (Matthew 26:30).

The value of our looking

The Bridegroom says:

> You have ravished my heart, my sister, my spouse, you have ravished my heart with one of your eyes, with one chain of your neck.
>
> How fair is your love, my sister, my spouse! how much better is your love than wine! and the smell of your ointments than all spices!
>
> Your lips, O my spouse, drop as the honeycomb: honey and milk are under your tongue; and the smell of your garments is as the smell of Lebanon.

Jesus calls the believing soul 'sister' and 'spouse' – concepts which are normally mutually exclusive, because it is an abomination to have your sister as your spouse. But the unique relationship between Jesus and a believing soul is typified in the Old Testament by the fact that Abraham took as his wife a girl who was also his half-sister.

The relationship between Jesus and the Christian can take many forms. Sometimes it is that of an older brother advising a younger sister; at other times it is the passionate love of a bridegroom towards a bride. One analogy on its own would be inadequate to express the variety of the relationship.

Even in the Old Testament, God speaking to Israel sometimes calls himself a father, sometimes a comforting mother and at other times a bridegroom, a husband or a friend. One and the same God – and so many analogies!

Jesus tells the bride, 'You have ravished my heart.' There is really no satisfactory translation of the Hebrew expression in the European languages. The nearest we could come would be to say something like, 'My love for you drove me out of my mind.' The Hebrew word for 'love' used here is a plural form – 'loves'. The bride loves him with intellectual love, with rational love and with passionate love.

The Son of God acknowledges that through love, he has become our prisoner. How does this happen? Then, as sometimes now, oriental girls veiled their faces. To be flirtatious they would lower their veil just a fraction, showing one eye, if they were near somebody in whom they had an interest. So the believing soul ravishes the heart of the Saviour with one of her eyes, with one of her glances.

It is written in the Old Testament that the Jews, bitten by serpents in the wilderness, had only to look at the brazen serpent erected by Moses in order to be healed. One look at Jesus is sufficient to bring a soul to salvation and to make him an heir of the eternal life.

How can a mere look have such huge results? It is because we ravish his heart. We take from his mind everything but ourselves. Through a single look, we inflame him with love. So great is the poweer of a loving look! God can thereby become ours.

Happy is the soul that loves. It takes God prisoner, and God listens to it in all things. You cannot obtain from God by mighty deeds what you can obtain from him by a single loving look.

A farmer was seen to spend many hours in church before the altar, but he never seemed to pray. When he was asked what he was doing, he said, 'I just kneel and look at God.' So it is that one single quality of the bride – one single loving look – secures God's whole heart. Let us likewise love men for a single quality we perceive in them, and close our eyes to all the rest which might be inadequate.

In the Old Testament the caresses of the truly faithful soul were more pleasant to God than all the incense which was offered to him in the Temple of Jerusalem.

The Bridegroom also tells the bride, 'honey and milk

are under your tongue.' The Jews endured forty years of hardship, to finally see the Promised Land flowing with milk and honey. After conquering Canaan, they fought hard to keep it. But all those years they already had the joyous realms of 'honey and milk' – right under their tongues. We all have the Promised Land the moment we stop looking for it in the far distance. It is there, in the power of our tongue. Our own bitter words bring us to hell. But confessing with the mouth that Jesus Christ is our Lord, brings us salvation.

A garden enclosed

The Bridegroom says:

> A garden enclosed is my sister, my spouse; a spring shut up, a fountain sealed.
> Your plants are an orchard of pomegranates, with pleasant fruits; camphire with spikenard,
> Spikenard and saffron; calumus and cinnamon, with all trees of frankincense; myrrh and aloes, with all the chief spices;
> A fountain of gardens, a well of living waters, and streams from Lebanon.
>
> (4:12-15)

Jeremiah predicted a time when the souls of Israel would be well-watered gardens. For the bride this is already accomplished; she is a well-defended and enclosed garden.

Using these images, Jesus praises her chastity. Nobody can enter a closed garden or draw water from a sealed fountain except the owner. When he does not come to visit her, the garden of the bride is locked. She knows that, just as a perfume bottle does not lose its fragrance if it is kept closed, neither does the soul which tends only to God lose the warmth of love and the power of virtue.

It is said of the resurrection Lord that he came to his disciples when the doors of their rooms were kept shut for fear of the Jews (John 20:19). If they kept their doors shut against those who could only kill them in this world, how much more should we be like locked doors for fear of the demons who can destroy our eternal life! To keep the doors locked – to be an enclosed garden – to be separated from the world – that is the proper state of your heart, if you wish Jesus to show himself to you.

We have to be wary and lock our doors against influences which are harmful to our souls. Spiritual enemies can quench the Spirit in us. They take God from us and spoil our intimacy with him, the divine solace and eternal life. Why should you be an open fountain, at everybody's disposal, so that men can spit in it or throw their garbage in? Is there anything that pleases you more than the presence of the Holy Spirit?

Our inner castle, where God's kingdom thrives, must be kept locked against the images of the outside world. We must ensure that the world remains outside, that it finds no foothold in us, so that we shall not be destroyed. Our imagination and our fantasies must be as beautiful as a locked garden. Certain things may be allowed to enter and others must be forbidden. God and the devil come with their gifts to the gate of this garden. God's gifts must be accepted, the devil's rejected.

God said to Cain, 'If you do not well, sin lies at the door. And unto you shall be his desire' (Genesis 4:7). In Revelation 3:20 Jesus says, 'Behold, I stand at the door, and knock: if any man hear my voice, and open the door, I will come in to him, and will sup with him, and he with me.'

The faithful soul desires that only the Lord shall enter. But the devil, knowing this, disguises himself as an angel of light. How can we distinguish between them? What must we do? We must keep our doors locked. We need to be an enclosed garden. The fact that our doors are locked is no hindrance to Jesus. He knows how to pass through locked doors.

Nobody has to be more righteous, more loving, than the bride in the Song of Solomon. She is alert when she lies on her bed: she hears the voice of the Beloved: 'Open to me, my sister, my love, my dove, my undefiled' (5:2). But she also knows that the devil can imitate the voice of Jesus. The many compliments make her especially suspicious.

Then she – who is sick of love for him, who has sought him for many nights, walking the lonely streets and marketplaces seeking the Beloved – now, when she hears the voice at the door, refuses to open it: 'I have put off my coat; how shall I put it on? I have washed my feet; how shall I defile them?' (5:3).

Jesus is pleased with her wise refusal, and exclaims in admiration, 'A garden enclosed is my sister, my spouse; a spring shut up, a fountain sealed' (4:12). The Jesus she refused is the true Jesus, because he does not become angry. He knows us. He sees us. He searches our hearts, and knows we are with him. He knows for what good motives we refuse him.

He also knows why we cannot be gardens forever closed. He knows our commitment brings us into contact with many sins, many cultures, many false religions and denials of God to which we would not be exposed if we remained permanently enclosed gardens. We cannot share our faith with others without also hearing their stories of wickedness in their lives and their arguments for other beliefs. It is unavoidable that some of this should seem alluring. There have been cases of missionaries falling into sin with those they were to bring to holiness.

The best thing is to avoid extremes. We must avoid being so enclosed that others will die because, like black holes, we emit no light. And we must avoid being so outgoing that we forget that without times of withdrawing into a quiet garden we cannot have a love-life with Jesus.

He praises the enclosed garden. The flowers and fruits mentioned are mostly exotic in Israel, and as such are types of the rare pleasures that the bride offers to the Bridegroom. She is a garden full of them. Originally the word for garden was *pardes*, a Persian word from which we derive 'paradise'. For him to come near the bride was the same happiness that we shall receive when we enter paradise, because the Church produces the most exquisite fruits for him. Where aloes grow, all the air is perfumed. The Church fills the air with the choice perfume of Jesus.

The bride is called 'a fountain of gardens, a well of living waters, and streams from Lebanon.' The rivers flowing out of Lebanon are very fast-flowing and crystal clear. So is the source of wisdom, which continually flows from the mouth of the bride. So are the rivers of living water, coming from her heart, which has become a temple of the Holy Spirit.

Only keep your heart as an enclosed garden, and Jesus will enter it with his burning love.

The privilege of enclosed gardens

Every 8th October the Russian Orthodox Church celebrates the birth of the seventeenth century saint, Tryphon of Viatsk. His enemies stripped him of his clothes, bound him and threw him in the snow. When they later went to retrieve the frozen corpse, they found instead a living body which was unusually warm. The snow around him had melted. In Rumanian prisons it was said that the same thing happened when they threw the Christian, Budu, naked into the snow. I myself have known many who were put into refrigerated cells at freezing temperatures and survived. Jesus entered through the locked doors of the cells, and the Christians filled them with songs of praise.

Freezing circumstances in your own life will not freeze you, if you are close to the burning fire of Godhead.

I once attended an evensong celebrated by Seraphim, the archbishop of the underground True Orthodox Church in the Soviet Union. He has led his church for thirty years, yet the Communists never discovered his whereabouts.

At that evensong, after he had chanted the first words – 'In the name of the Father, and of the Son and of the Holy Ghost' – the whole congregation was already in tears. I had heard and said those words thousands of times. But as Seraphim said them I realized as never before the dramatic truth that all we have of God is his name to call upon. During the fourteen years of my imprisonment, 'Father' was only a name to my son. He was deprived of the reality of a father-son relationship. We are in the same position with the heavenly Father, but we have the comfort of knowing that he is a loving Father. His Son died for us; his Holy Spirit guides us. The whole message was revealed to me in the way Seraphim chanted the words. Several people in the congregation asserted that they could see a luminous being conducting the service with him, although he was alone. I believe that anyone who commits his soul to the act of imparting the gospel (1 Thessalonians 2:8) has angels at his side at the altar.

This is the privilege of men who live in enclosed gardens; who allow none to enter their intimacy; who shun all influence. The right influence, the Bridegroom himself, can leap over hindrances.

Awake, winds

The bride says:

'Awake, O north wind; and come, south; blow upon my garden, that the spices thereof may flow out. Let my beloved come into his garden, and eat his pleasant fruits.' The Bridegroom replies: 'I am come into my garden, my sister, my spouse; I have gathered my myrrh with my spice; I have eaten my honeycomb with my honey; I have drunk my wine with my milk: eat, O friends, drink, yea, drink abundantly, O beloved' (4:16–5:1).

Though she is so appreciated by him the bride whispers into his ear that she still needs to make preparations befor presenting herself to him. The girls who had to enter the presence of the earthly king Ahasuerus first had to beautify themselves for twelve months: six months with oil of myrrh and six with sweet odours (Esther 1:12). How much more so should girls who must present themselves before the heavenly king beautify themselves. Therefore the bride calls the winds.

The north wind represents the punishments of God. The south wind, opening the pores of the leaves to allow them to exhale their sweet fragrance, represents the comforts of God. Both are signs of his love, and both are needed so that the garden of the bride may spread her perfume.

The Church has a rich share of punishments and comforts. Above all, it has the privilege of being blown upon by the wind of the Holy Spirit, which descended upon the disciples at Pentecost. That was a fulfilment of the bride's prayer.

The north wind blows with unprecedented fierceness upon the Christians in Communist countries, whose rulers have a long record of crime. In Addis Abeba, the capital of Communist Ethiopia, the prisons are filled with Christians and Moslems. The torturers use Cuban-made manacles which can be rapidly tightened until the bones break. A prisoner in the Andijane jail in Uzbekistan, USSR, reported: 'The inmates are beaten to death or put in straightjackets. The chief torturer is Umayukulov. Those who suffer for their convictions are put in cells together with bandits, who sodomize them.'

In Czechoslovakia 3,000 nuns were prisoners in their

convents, which had been made into slave labour camps. The number of priests and monks who have had to endure the same fate is not known. Since books with a religious content cannot be printed legally in Czechoslovakia, secret printing presses have been set up at enormous risk. Such presses are also run in Russia, China and other Communist countries. When they are discovered the printers go to prison.

Tito, the late president of Yugoslavia, was the murderer of one in seven of the country's priests, and of countless residents of convents. Also on his conscience is the death of Cardinal Stepinac, who personally protected 7,000 children and defended Jews and Serbians during World War II.

At the end of that war the Soviet army occupying East Germany killed the priests Sonsalla, Demczak and Goerlich. Innumerable girls were raped. Some of them were nuns. Brutes of the same quality still control the Communist countries.

All these crimes have been surpassed by the holocaust in Cambodia. Around two million people were killed by the Communists. Men with university degrees were eradicated. The wearing of spectacles was made a crime punishable by death, because it indicated the ability to read. Of 500 physicians, only 57 are still alive. The children of undesirables were chained together and buried alive. Scarcely any children below the age of five remained. In the beginning, no local men had the strength to unload the relief parcels from abroad.

Yakunin, the Russian Orthodox priest, was imprisoned for protesting against church leaders who compromised with Communism, that is, brides of Christ who are in bed with his enemies. He wrote: 'Authority in the church belongs to Christ alone who obtained it by shedding His precious blood. The church is His holy spouse, His living body. Whoever permits power-seekers to interfere with the eternal life of the church, abandons Christ's bride to corruption.'

Men like this would be able to agree with these words of Hudson Taylor, founder of the China Inland Mission:

> I was envied by some, despised by many, hated perhaps by others, often blamed for things I had nothing to do with; an innovator of what have become established rules of missionary practice, working in many respects without precedence and with few experienced helpers; often sick in body as well as perplexed in mind, and embarrassed by circumstance.
>
> Had not the Lord been especially gracious to me, had not my mind been sustained by the conviction that the work is His and He is with me, I must have fainted and broken down. But the battle is the Lord's – and He will conquer.

In Gardenas, in Byelorussia, USSR, Communists have destroyed a fourteenth-century Gothic church. The same thing happened with the splendid temple of Vidzial. In Varanavas, women tried to prevent demolition of the church by throwing themselves in front of the bulldozers. Such devotion to the very end is the highest pleasure that you can give to Jesus. The bride of Christ under persecution gives him that pleasure in the worst possible circumstances. She has only one purpose. To make Jesus joyous.

Holy fantasy

She calls upon the Bridegroom to enter into her soul: 'Let my beloved come into his garden, and eat his pleasant fruits.' When she called upon the Lord, he replied, 'Here I am.' His response was immediate. He came in to her and she spent a splendid bridal night with him. He found his delight in her, and remembers her caresses now with joy; 'I have come into my garden, my sister, my spouse, I have gathered my myrrh and my spice; I have eaten my honeycomb with my honey; I have drunk my wine with my milk.' These are all different descriptions of the pleasure she has given him. Jesus, having known his bride, soars on peaks of joy, because those delights were so richly varied and full of beauty.

Normally, people do not eat the comb with the honey; neither do they drink a mixture of wine and milk. But the delights which Christ finds in the Church are unique delights. She does 'more than others' (Matthew 5:47).

And the bridegroom calls his friends: 'Eat, O friends; drink, yes, drink abundantly, O beloved.' These men are not like the bride. They do not know the joys of intimate fellowship with Jesus, but only participate, through his benevolence, in others' privileges.

When you are invited to a meal, those who invite you do not always wish you well. There may be small-talk at their meals, and backbiting afterwards. But the invitation which Jesus extends is sincere and comes whole-heartedly. Jesus calls us all to his banquet, to the joy of seeing sinners converted, and he calls us to attend the wedding feast of the Bridegroom and the bride. Blessed are those invited to this banquet! God commands the guests to eat and drink abundantly. Only one greater happiness exists, and that is to be part of the Body of the bride herself.

Atheists reject the wedding feast as fantasy. A courier who smuggled Bibles into a Communist country was told, 'We don't accept books like these; they are fairy tales.' The courier replied, 'Don't you have fairy tale books in your country?' To this, the customs officer had no reply.

The courier then said to him, 'There is nothing wrong in works of fantasy, if the fantasy is sanctified and is only employed in the embellishment of true facts.'

The union between Christ and the believer is such a true

fact. We can embellish it. Fantasy is a beautiful gift of God. In the first Greek translation of Zechariah, it is written 'The Lord made fantasy' (Zechariah 10:1). It is a product of imaginative creation.

Christian hymns are the product of saintly fantasy. For example, consider '*There is a fountain filled with blood, drawn from Emmanuel's veins.*' The blood of Jesus coagulated in his hands and feet when he was crucified. Otherwise he would have bled to death within minutes. Only trickles of blood oozed from his wounds. But fantasy enriches reality. The sinner sees before him a deep fountain of cleansing blood into which he can plunge. There is more spiritual reality in the fantasy than in the strict historic event.

Without fantasies, there would be no achievement in life. Technology, medicine and art would all wither away. Science fiction anticipated science fact. Flights of fantasy preceded flights into space. Each step forward begins as a step of fantasy which later becomes a reality.

The pleasures of the union between bride and Bridegroom, and the final wedding feast, are surely the product of fantasy; but when the reality takes place, they will be seen as a fantastic description of a real event. Christians believe in this invitation to the wedding feast of the Lamb. They believe in the inebriating joys of drinking abundantly at his feast. Therefore they gladly bear their crosses.

In the village of Martuk in the Aktiubinskaia region of the Soviet republic of Kazakh, the school director – a man called Goroh – threatened a fourteen-year-old Christian girl, Arganessa Tissen. He said that if she continued to win souls to Christ, he would authorize children to put a rope round her neck and hang her on the spot. He compelled Christian children to crawl on all fours, in a travesty of kneeling at prayer. He called them 'Fascists'.

The Baptist Anatoli Y. Khailo was imprisoned on a false charge of raping and beating a girl, even though somebody else has already confessed to this crime. The girl's mother has also admitted that the prosecutor instructed her to give false evidence against Khailo. Just like Joseph in the Old Testament, who was imprisoned on a charge of attempted rape even though he was holy and refused to sin, Khailo must suffer.

This ugly side of life can distress us. But we know about the wedding feast to which we are all invited. We do not look merely on the rain, but on their iridescent rainbow.

The Baptist Church in Belgorod, after enumerating many facts about the persecution, writes: 'We thank God that He found us worthy of such an honour. We pray that He will give us all the strength not to be shaken, because the hour of the Lord's coming is near. May the Lord bless us, and teach us to understand the shrewd methods of His enemies.'

The Christians of Belgrorod are looking forward to the coming wedding feast. Though the banquet is a product of holy fantasy, it is a picture of future reality.

In Solomon's Song even erotic fantasy is sanctified. By that means he describes the coming drunkenness of love which the bride will experience in the embrace of the heavenly Bridegroom. This holy fantasy has helped many Christians to win through in Communist prisons.

Many people are attracted to so much that is ugly, to things worse than reality. We who are Christians are attracted to the beautiful, to the righteous, to the real, expressed in the most gorgeous images.

≈ *Chapter 5* ≈

A sad chapter in the life of the bride

The bride says:

> I sleep, but my heart wakes: it is the voice of my beloved that knocks, saying, 'Open to me, my sister, my love, my dove, my undefiled: for my head is filled with dew, and my locks with drops of the night.'
>
> I have put off my coat; how shall I put it on? I have washed my feet; how shall I defile them?
>
> My beloved put in his hand by the hole of the door, and my bowels were moved for him.
>
> I rose up to open to my beloved; and my hands dropped with myrrh, and my fingers with sweet smelling myrrh, upon the handles of the lock.
>
> I open to my beloved; but my beloved had withdrawn himself, and was gone: my soul failed when he spoke: I sought him but I could not find him; I called him, but he gave me no answer.
>
> (5:2–6)

She sleeps; but he who is in her heart never sleeps nor slumbers. Just when the bride has fallen asleep, the word was fulfilled: 'Behold, I stand at the door and knock.' She hears the Beloved's voice.

Those who are awake must seek Jesus; but he comes himself to the one who is asleep. There is not the slightest rebuke in his words, no anger at finding he asleep. He says only, 'Open to me, my sister, my dove, my undefiled.' The *Talmud* says, 'Open to God a door as big as the point of a needle, and He will enter with a cart full of blessings.' How can one not let in someone who begs you, 'Open to me, sleeper with beautiful eyelids'? How can one refuse entry to somebody who says not one angry word, though such words would be justified, but only says that he, the ruler of heaven and earth, has nowhere to lay his head? Where will he rest, if his bride does not call him? His hair is filled with dew because he has spent the night in the fields, without a roof over his head.

However, the bride prevaricates. She will not open to him at once: 'I have put off my coat . . . I have washed my feet,' she says. But if she has put her coat off, she can either receive Jesus naked, or she can make haste to clothe herself again. If she has put off the garment of sin, she should never put it on again; but as for other garments, she can put them on in no time. And what sort of reply is this, that she has washed her feet and fears to defile them again? She knows that Jesus washed his disciples' feet. He will do it for her also. She is merely prevaricating.

And then he puts his hand by the hole of the door. When we offer excuses, the grace of God tries to force the entrance. But even he cannot open the door of the heart. That door can only be opened from the inside.

It was only then that pity moved her. If you can't manage any other sentiment for Jesus, at least have pity for one who has been hurt so much.

When she rose to open to the Beloved, her hands dripped with myrrh, which was on the handles of the lock. Oriental keyholes are usually very large, and he must have poured perfume on the handles from outside, out of a bottle he had brought for her. When she put her fingers on the handle, this perfume dripped from them.

She opens to the Beloved; but he has gone. He has withdrawn himself. She did not open at the first knock, and now he cannot be found. How many reasons for sadness we give ourselves, when we neglect opportunities that God offers!

She remembers now how sweet his voice was. Her soul had failed when he spoke. The Vulgate, the first Latin translation of the Bible, says here, 'My soul melted when he spoke.' That is how one can tell that it is the Lord who is speaking. Disciples of Jesus who talked with him after the Resurrection said to each other, 'Did not our hearts burn within us, while he talked with us along the way, and while he opened to us the Scriptures?' (Luke 24:32). It is always a thrilling event when the Lord speaks to his souls.

But human beings are strange. The bride fainted when she heard him; but she did not open the door. Afterwards she seeks him and does not find him. She calls for him, but he does not answer. It would all have been unnecessary, had she opened the door at once. There are times in the life of a man or woman when answers from Jesus cannot be obtained anymore. Why did they delay in answering the door? Was it because they had put off their clothes? The clothes of righteousness should never be put off.

A young man was married to a girl by a priest of the outlawed Uniate Catholic Church of the Ukraine. The Communists arrested her, and told her husband that his new wife would be raped by scores of soldiers if he did not denounce the priest. At that moment he should have opened his heart to Jesus, the Saviour who was ready to suffer for God's glory. Opening his heart at that moment of tragic dilemma, the young Christian would have known the simple truth that a Christian is never a denunciator, no matter what the circumstances. But he did not. He gave in. He denounced the priest who was in hiding. When his wife heard of this she tried to commit suicide. His mother died of a broken heart, and the priest went to prison. The husband later confessed his guilt, and died after valiantly protecting an innocent thirteen-year-old girl from the Communists.

Others who have allowed Jesus to enter their hearts have

acquired his courage. In Vietnam, everyone must have a permit to leave his quarters. Permits are not available to pastors. But they do leave their quarters, to answer calls from sick parishioners or simply to preach the gospel elsewhere. When caught, some were punished by being made to kneel in front of their doors for a whole week. So they knelt, and kneeling, they made plans about how they would propagate the gospel when they were allowed to rise to their feet. If they were caught again they risked new punishments, perhaps prison or even death. The pastors Nguyen van Thang and Nguyen van Nam died in Vietnamese jails.

All church property has been confiscated: schools, seminaries, universities and orphanages. However, God's children continue their work.

The Communists demanded that nuns working in hospitals should perform abortions. They refused, and so had to leave their work.

Since May 1975, 247 Catholic priests have been killed, and hundreds more have been sent to re-education camps, from which not all returned. The Evangelical clergy met the same fate.

In Uganda under the dictator Idi Amin, Christians, as well as political opponents of the regime and common criminals, were imprisoned in the concentration camps Mabira and Namamve. These prisoners were not fed at all. They lived by the law of the jungle; the strong ate the weak. Obviously, the Christians were among those eaten. It is an old African custom that such victims are not killed before being eaten; one piece after another is stripped from the living body. This information is taken from the records of an International Commission of Jurists at the United Nations.

Christians bore this with faithfulness. In their suffering, many must have cried to him and had the same experience as the bride In Solomon's Song: 'I called to him but he gave no answer.' Great faith is tested by long periods of waiting. But in the end, there is no such thing as an unanswered prayer. The answer will surely come. It might not be the answer that we desired, but it will surely be the best answer for us.

Bad pastors

The bride complains: 'The watchmen that went about the city found me, they smote me, they wounded me; the keepers of the walls took away my veil from me' (5:7). The watchmen of the city represent the pastors of the Church. Instead of helping the bride to find her Beloved, they beat her and wound her and take away her veil. Jesus foresaw that some of his pastors would begin to persecute his servants. They would care only about eating and drinking and enjoying themselves. In olden times many great persecutions against believers were unleashed by priests who, under the pretext of defending the Church, mistreated the children of God who were meek and spiritual.

The priest Eli rebuked holy Anna for drunkenness, but he had not one word of reproach for his wicked sons. Many pastors have grieved the hearts of the righteous. Even good pastors commit this sin. So the bride walks about, saddened by her own conscience and now by her pastors.

Prisoners in Communist prisons do not only suffer from the persecutor; they suffer also from betrayal by the leadership of their denominations. At the exact time that Pentecostalists in Rumania were being beaten by the police, the official leaders of the Pentecostal Union of Rumania, who are received as brethren at conferences in the Free World, congratulated the Rumanian government in the columns of the Communist press for the 'full liberty' it bestows. They sent a letter to all the churches, obliging them to refrain from preaching about God's judgement, because the Communists do not like to hear this subject spoken about.

In Red China during the Cultural Revolution, opponents of the regime (and all Christians were automatically defined as such) had to kneel for ten minutes of self-examination in front of a portrait of Mao, and slap themselves on the face ten times each morning before entering their workplace, and again in the evening before they left. They were singled out to clean the lavatories. With heads shaved, they were tied up and dragged away for physical punishment.

At that time some Christian leaders in the West were praising the Maoist regime as a fulfilment of God's kingdom. Later, the Chinese Communists themselves discovered the crimes committed under Mao. However, some pastors had covered them up.

Sick of love

The bride says, 'I charge you, O daughters of Jerusalem, if you find my beloved, that you tell him, that I am sick of love' (5:8). Beaten by the watchmen on the walls, the bride is unable to continue her search. She demands of others that they should pray for her. She uses third parties as intercessors on her behalf. The lover uses all means possible to make contact with the Beloved.

'If you find my beloved' – she does not name him. A powerful love always supposes that everybody else loves the Beloved as well. She gives them a command: 'Tell him that I am sick of love.' You can tell when someone is sick from love, when that person cannot be dissuaded further from doing and suffering all things for the Beloved. It is written, 'You shall love the Lord your God with all your heart, and with all your soul, and with all your might' (Deuteronomy 6:5). Have you known what it is like to be love-sick?

You may well know what sea-sickness is. There is also such a thing as love-sickness. Do you know it? Do you know what it is to love to madness, to love to a paroxysm of love? This is love which, instead of drawing on its own large resources, demands even more love. It is better to have this dissatisfied love for Jesus, than a satisfied love for the world. This is the message that her messengers are to bring to him: that though she has been neglected, she still loves.

She does not ask him to come. She only tells him her pain. Here we are taught that prayers should only mention one's needs without making explicit demands; then he, knowing our needs, will do what he thinks best. There are many such prayers in the Bible. For example, Martha's prayer: 'Behold, he whom you love is sick' (John 11:3). This prayer ony speaks of the need. The mother of our Lord at the wedding in Cana says only this much: 'They have no wine' (John 2:3).

Prayers which only express the need have a unique beauty. He is the Master. You tell him only the situation. He knows better than we do what needs to be done in such circumstanccs. He feels more pity when he sees the beloved soul suffering with resignation, selflessly. Only speak your sorrow, without demanding what you think is necessary. The bride sends messages to tell him only, 'I am sick of love.'

We have many examples of this sort of love in the persecuted Church in the Communist world today. Valya was a twelve-year-old Russian girl. One day the director of her school decided that she should become a member of the Communist children's movement known as the Pioneers. She refused. Her refusal was invalid, because the director had legal rights over her such as only parents have in the Free World.

Enrolment day arrived. The chosen candidates stood before a table on which lay three-pointed Pioneer scarves. One by one the girls stepped forward to don the scarf and take the oath.

'Valya Vastchenko,' called the director. 'Valya, step forward. Take the oath.'

Valya's mouth stayed tightly shut.

'Say the oath, Valya! . . . Very well. I will read it in your name.' The director pointed to two other girls. 'Place the scarf around her neck as I read.'

He began. 'I, Valya, pioneer of the USSR, promise before my comrade-patriots who decide the question of my admission to the organization, that I will stand firmly for the cause of Lenin and the victory of Communism. I promise . . .'

His next words were drowned as Valya burst out in prayer to God and began to sing a hymn: '*We will stand firm for the Faith, for Christ, following His example.*'

That child knew from the experience of many others that she had destroyed her future career for the rest of her life. She knew she might be put into an atheistic boarding school. She knew that her parents might be put into prison and might even die there, but she did not rationalize. She loved Jesus to a paroxysm, so she could not do other than what she did.

Thomas Aquinas was discussing the Song of Solomon when he died. On his death, the song that he wrote entitled, *I adore You*, expressing his love and desire for Jesus, became especially relevant:

> *Jesus, whom for the present, veiled I see,*
> *What I so long for, Oh! vouchsafe to me;*
> *That I may see Your beauteous face unfolding*
> *And may be blessed, Your glory in beholding.*

The bride is sick of love, which means that she suffers. We have to defend our faith against the heresy of a Christianity without suffering, without a cross. Let me quote from typical sermons as preached frequently on American television.

'If a man can stand totally in the presence of Almighty

God, he will never be sick.' Thousands are sick of tuberculosis contracted through hunger in Communist prisons. Others were maimed by torture. Others went mad.

'The grace of God brings about his blessings in the spiritual and the material realm.' Prisoners in the Communist camps shiver in the cold, their families are fired from their jobs and have no money to buy bread for their children. Their goods are confiscated. Where is the material blessing?

'As his children, it is not our place to be in the maelstrom of the storm that swirls around us. We do not have to be buffetted around by all the torments that afflict the world. Even when trouble comes, the sunlight of God is shining and there is peace upon us.' This celebrated preacher doesn't seem to have heard about the dark night of the soul through which well-known saints have passed. I dispute the claim that Christians are at peace in all circumstances.

The bride in Solomon's Song knows deep peace, but she also knows grave torments and sickness.

What does our beloved have more than others?

The bride is asked: 'What is your beloved more than another beloved, O fairest among women? what is your beloved more than another beloved, that you so charge us?' She replies:

> My beloved is white and ruddy, the chiefest among ten thousand.
>
> His head is as the most fine gold, his locks are bushy, and black as a raven.
>
> His eyes are as the eyes of doves by the rivers of waters, washed with milk, and fitly set.
>
> His cheeks are as a bed of spices, as sweet flowers; his

lips like lilies, dropping sweet smelling myrrh.

His hands are as gold rings set with the beryl: his belly is as bright ivory overlaid with sapphires.

His legs are as pillars of marble, set upon sockets of fine gold: his countenance is as Lebanon, excellent as the cedars.

His palate is sweetness and all desires: yes, he is altogether lovely. This is my beloved, and this is my friend, O daughters of Jerusalem.

(5:9–16)

The world does not know the beauty of the Bridegroom, but can see the beauty of the bride, of the Church. She really is the 'fairest among women.' The world wonders about her love for Jesus, and asks her, 'What does your Beloved have more than others?' Rabbi Solomon Iarchi, a celebrated commentator, writes: 'Thus the nations ask the Israelites: What is your God more than all gods, that you are burned up with hunger for him like this?'

She answers with a model sermon. It is a sermon preached by a soul that loves to a paroxysm. It is not a boring exposition of Bible verses. It is a description of what the Beloved is. Isaiah preached in the same way:

He is despised and rejected of men; a man of sorrows, and acquainted with grief: and we hid as it were our faces from him; he was despised, and we esteemed him not.

Surely he has borne our griefs, and carried our sorrows: yet we did esteem him stricken, smitten of God, and afflicted.

But he was wounded for our transgressions, he was bruised for our iniquities: the chastisement of our peace was upon him; and with his stripes we are healed.

All we like sheep have gone astray; we have turned every one to his own way; and the Lord has laid on him the iniquity of us all.

He was oppressed, and he was afflicted, yet he opened

not his mouth: he is brought as a lamb to the slaughter, and as a sheep before the shearers is dumb, so he opened not his mouth.

He was taken from prison and from judgement: and who shall declare his generation? For he was cut off out of the land of the living; for the transgression of my people he was stricken.

And he made his grave with the wicked, and with the rich in his death; because he had done no violence, neither was there any deceit in his mouth.

Yet it pleased the Lord to bruise him; he has put him to grief; when he shall make his soul an offering for sin, he shall see his seed, he shall prolong his days, and the pleasure of the Lord shall prosper in his hand.

He shall see the travail of his soul, and shall be satisfied; by his knowledge shall my righteous servant justify many; for he shall bear their iniquities.

(Isaiah 53:3–11)

So also did the apostle John preach:

And so in the midst of the seven candlesticks [I saw] one like unto the Son of Man, clothed with a garment down to the foot, and girt about the paps with a golden girdle.

His head and his hairs were white like wool, as white as snow; and his eyes were as a flame of fire;

And his feet like unto fine brass, as if they burned in a furnace; and his voice as the sound of many waters.

And he had in his right hand seven stars: and out of his mouth went a sharp two-edged sword: and his countenance was as the sun shines in his strength.

(Revelation 1:13–16)

With Isaiah we find Jesus' state of humility described; with John the Evangelist, a description of His glory. The bride describes his beauty. She has had his body lying near her, she has caressed it, she knows it.

Yet the description of the Bridegroom is very far from reality. The body is too shiny. The beauty of the young man seems more that of a gilded statue than that of a human being. It is probable that she is comparing him to a work of Egyptian art. Ancient Egyptian sculpture was colourfully painted, and the flesh of males was painted red. Therefore she calls him 'ruddy'. (In 7:2 we find concerning the bride the words, 'Your belly is like an heap of wheat set about with lilies'; this image is explained by the fact that female sculptures were always painted yellow, the colour of wheat.)

The Egyptians also made bronze figures inlaid with gold, silver and copper. Surely we are reminded of this when the legs are described as columns of alabaster and the feet as gold. It was a common device in Egyptian statues. To the bride, these features represent stability and grandeur.

Here the young man's legs are described in their entirety; in 7:1, only the feet of the girl are mentioned. In old Egyptian art, the legs of males were unclothed, whereas the legs of females were never revealed except in the cases of children, dancers or dolls.

What is said here about the Messiah has a deeper spiritual significance. He is white because he is God and, though a man, without sin. He is red from the many whippings and sufferings he has endured. He is white, to show sinners that their sins too, can become white. But the red also warns them of the coming vengeance of God against sinners.

'His eyes are as the eyes of doves.' In jail I had the opportunity to observe the lives of doves. They nested in the prison walls. I never saw fierceness nor fury in their eyes. They were always loving. This verse reminds me of them.

Of the Bridegroom's hands, the bride says (according to the Authorized Version), 'they are as golden rings set with the beryl' – a precious stone. The Hebrew says, 'set in Tarshish'. This is a strange word, for in the Bible it can mean either a personal name, a kind of ship or a country. Nobody knows for sure where the place called Tarshish was.

Here the use of this word teaches us to see God's loving hand in what is achieved by human hands, in material objects and in great events involving whole nations.

Modest brides do not describe their beloved's belly to their girlfriends. The bride sets aside the normal conventions of decency and does so. She wants to suggest to every soul that Jesus can be known in the most intimate embraces. What needs to be concealed? His naked body was displayed in public on the Cross.

She ends her description by saying, 'He is altogether lovely' or, 'He is all desires.' Every desire of a bride can find fulfilment in him. 'This is my beloved, and this is my friend.' She is sure he is her beloved, though for a time he left her.

We see how beautiful Jesus is in the eyes of his bride, by the description of him in Christian poetry, and by the works of the great sculptors and painters. We also see his beauty in the heavenly music composed in his honour by renowned composers.

The persecuted Christians know his beauty. The pupil Atkociunaite told her teacher in Soviet Lithuania, 'I don't care what you do to me. On the eve of Easter I will remain the whole night in adoration in the church.' If he were not beautiful, nobody would spend a whole night looking at him in adoration!

In a book published secretly by the Orthodox Underground Church, the author writes:

> A man travelled on the shores of the Azov sea. He saw fishermen at work. The thought came to him, 'If the sea contained no fish, nobody would be fishing. Nobody goes to a well that has no water. If there were no grace in the church, nobody would go there.
>
> A fool can go into a cellar and proclaim that there is no sun in the universe. Truly, for those in cellars there is none. So, there is no God, for those who are in the darkness of God-denial and evil.'

Living under fierce persecution, this author writes, 'God is richness, fullness of life, love. All beauty, all power, all good, is only in God.' He writes thus, a member of a church whose people are jailed, tortured and killed.

The Orthodox priest Nicholas Ivassiuk was assassinated in Tchardjow, Turkmenia, on 5 December 1978. Six men in police uniforms entered his house. Next morning Ivassiuk was found dead. His eyes had been gouged out (just as happened with the Baptist Victor Sedletskii), and his body had been burned by cigarettes and red-hot irons. There were also numerous lacerations. He had been finished off with two bullets through the head. Such things belong to the ritual of Satanist sects. The crime was perpetrated on the eve of the Feast of St Nicholas, whose name the priest bore, as a calculated mockery of the saint. Ivassiuk left five daughters.

And yet from such a place of cruelty and sorrow, the Orthodox Underground Church publishes writings full of joy, jubilation and adoration of the beauty of Jesus! They know what that beauty is. They have seen him.

Michaela, a Rumanian Orthodox nun, like all Orthodox and Catholic Christians, believed that the Communion bread and wine really are the body and blood of our Lord. Every time she looked at the Sacrament, she saw his intoxicating beauty. When the police took over the Vladimireshti convent, she protected the altar with her own body. For this she was thrown into prison and mistreated beyond description. But from her solitary cell she tapped out the gospel in Morse code through the wall to her fellow-prisoners until she died. She had seen his beauty, and would not give up sharing her love for him.

≈ *Chapter 6* ≈

'Whither is your beloved gone?'

The bride is asked, 'Whither is your beloved gone, O fairest among women? Whither is your beloved turned aside? That we may seek him with you.' She replies, 'My beloved is gone down into his garden, to the beds of spices, to feed in the gardens, and to gather lilies' (6:1-2). Now that the girls have heard from her what makes her Beloved greater than any other, they also seek him. It is enough that one soul should seek Jesus in utter sincerity; then others will join in the search for him. Thus the girls now ask, 'Whither is your beloved gone?'

The bride knows that she is going to have to give good directions to those who ask. She is inspired; she gives a remarkable reply: 'My beloved is gone down.' For anyone who does not know Jesus, these are incomprehensible words. The celebrated Rabbi ben Ezra wrote this commentary on the text: 'This – of the One who ascended on high? He is said to gather lilies, because He dwells with the angels who are the righteous ones.' In the same way, most believers who have lost Jesus do not find him, because they think that now that they have fallen, he is far above them. But he did not ascend. He went down. He descended far below the level to which they have fallen, so as to be able to meet them in their misery. The bride who fell into sin by refusing to receive him in her home when he knocked on the door, now knows that 'He has gone down.'

In the beginning, God created man after his own image. When we lost that image, God came down and took upon himself the image of of man. He became incarnate, in a body like that of sinners. That is the way he always deals with us. If we cannot ascend to him, he descends to us. As ours sins increase, so does his grace. Because we cannot be saints, he puts himself on the same level as the sinners. That is the only way in which continual fellowship with him is made possible.

Encounters with Communists do not only create heroes of the faith. Many believers fall away. In Rhodesia, Communist terrorists kidnapped Simon Chengeta, a black Member of Parliament and a Christian. They forced his son, Steven, to beat him to death. The son, who bears the name of Christianity's first martyr, could have refused. Probably the result would have been that they would have hacked him to death alongside his father, using somebody else to do the deed. But Steven did not want to die. So he fell away from the faith and became a parricide.

It is a privilege to become a hero by choosing to suffer instead of making the Son of God bleed. Those who make the right choice have the joy of loving and forgiving even their torturers. But not all make the right choice.

In Addis Ababa, the Communists arrested a couple with their older children. The children under six were left behind in their home. Nobody dared to bring them even a crust of bread. That might have been considered a crime punishable by death. Christ teaches us to help, even when the circumstances put our lives at risk. I have known German Christians who helped Jews, and Jewish Christians who later helped Germans, when they were persecuted by the Soviets, even though the punishment for such acts of love was death. In the case of that Ethiopian family, Christians opted to fall away from the law of love and from Christ. The children died of hunger. That falling away was absolute for those who believed that the pure Jesus is far above the fallen or backsliding sinner. But those who believed that Jesus had come down, found the way back to him.

Once I shared a cell with two Uniate bishops. Under torture they had 'confessed' to being spies, black marketeers, and collaborators with the pre-revolutionary police. They 'confessed' that they had denounced Communists and had caused their arrest. Their tears never ceased. (It is said of the apostle Peter, that to the end of his days he wept whenever a cock crowed.)

The bishops constantly reproached themselves for their lack of heroism. They did not know how heroic their 'confessions' were. It was not the heroism of those who never give in, but heroism it was; a heroism of the fallen who know that though they are brought low, Christ went lower still, down to utter despair. So they found the courage to acknowledge their sinfulness – something rare among church leaders.

In Rumania, the Communists killed a Baptist pastor. At first a promising teacher, he later became an informer for the Secret Police. One of the pieces of information he passed on to the police concerned a secret meeting I had with a French Christian in Rumania. Everyone was suspicious of him. The brethren shunned him. He had no peace in his heart: he know that what he was doing was wrong.

He was astonished to find himself invited to the Lausanne Conference on Evangelism. After all, he was widely known to be a Communist agent. Once arrived in Switzerland, he criticized the true Christians in Rumania as lawbreakers; but all the time he could not understand why the pastors from the Free World, who had no obligations to the Secret Police, did not contradict him. Why were neither he nor the other Judases blamed?

In an attempt to ease his conscience, he confessed to a Western Christian publisher that he was working for the Communist Secret Police. The publisher smelt a good story and offered him an advance on a book. He was disappointed; he had hoped that this fellow-Christian would set him back on the right path.

He had to return to Rumania in the end. He was determined to repent. Soon he broke off all relations with the Police. They retaliated by staging a car 'accident' in which he was killed.

But he had understood that Jesus has gone down, far below the depths to which he himself had sunk. He died at peace with the Lord, thanks to the prayers, love and forgiveness of the Underground Church.

A faithful Bridegroom

The bride says, 'My beloved is gone down into his garden, to the beds of spices, to feed in the gardens, and to gather lilies. I am my beloved's, and my beloved is mine: he feeds among the lilies' (6:2–3). He who loves gardens and flowers has gone down into his garden to the bed of spices, which typify the various denominations. He picks lilies (spiritual believers) from them all. These keep their trust in him. They say, 'I am my beloved's, and my beloved is mine.' The bride retained this trust even though for a time he forsook her. God has sworn that he will be faithful. He will not lie to the disciples of David's Son. Our Bridegroom is always faithful.

Ion Cazacu was one of my best friends. During the Nazi occupation of Rumania he risked his life by 'stealing' Jewish children from the ghettoes. The Jewish Christians in Iashi were in danger of death. Already, 11,000 Jews had been killed. The rest were not allowed to leave the city. Then a friendly official was persuaded at my request to issue warrants of arrest against all Hebrew Christians. As a result they were able to travel in comfortable train compartments as 'prisoners', guarded by Cazacu, who was armed. Once they arrived safely in Bucharest, the order of arrest was torn up and the prisoners were brought to my house.

Cazacu and his wife were also the only people who succeeded in entering heavily guarded prisons with carloads of food for the hungry Christians in detention there. That is the sort of life lived by men who know that Christ is always faithful.

In Rhodesia, Communist guerrillas killed forty Catholic, Pentecostal and Salvationist missionaries, along with their families. The victims – a three-week-old baby among them – were beaten to death with hammers, bayonets and axes. Mrs Pickering, the mother of one of the dead, said: 'We have prayed that God may forgive our enemies. There is no bitterness in our hearts.'

Tremendous things are happening in Poland. Those fed by Jesus among lilies organized, for the first time in world history, a strike of 600,000 workers brandishing such weapons as prayers, Christian hymns, and Holy Communion. They occupied the factories, but there were no violent words or deeds. The leaders were motivated by a Christian spirit. Their chief demands were full religious liberty, the Church's right to time on television and radio and the right to publish. The striking workers made it possible for the anti-Communist Cardinal Wyszinsky to preach on television after thirty years of prohibition.

A new phase of world history was opened by the Christian Lech Walesa, the Polish strike leader. A man powerful because of God's deep peace, he risked his life and his liberty. He did not remain an obscure private soldier in the Christian struggle. He realised that officers and generals were needed. He developed the necessary spiritual qualities, and God promoted him to a high rank.

Jesus is the only shepherd who feeds his flock in gardens, among lilies. That is something no other shepherd would do! But we expect the unusual from him.

Beautiful as Tirzah

The Bridegroom says:

> You are beautiful, my love, as Tirzah, comely as Jerusalem, terrible as an army with banners.
>
> Turn away your eyes from me, for they have overcome me: your hair is as a flock of goats that appear from Gilead.
>
> Your teeth are as a flock of sheep that go up from washing, whereof every one bears twins, and there is not one barren among them.
>
> As a piece of pomegranate are your temples within your locks.
>
> (6:4–7)

The Bridegroom compares his bride with the capitals of the two Jewish kingdoms: Tirzah – which means in Hebrew, 'the pleasant' – was the capital of Israel until Omri built Samaria; and Jerusalem was the capital of Judah.

Faithful souls are sometimes sad, and ask themselves, 'Do I deserve to become an inhabitant of the heavenly Jerusalem?' What a senseless question! In the eyes of the Bridegroom we are as pleasant and beautiful as Jerusalem itself. Therefore, naturally, that is where we should be.

The beauty of the bride makes her 'terrible as an army', with the banners under which it advances to victory. We overcome the world by faith; and with our beauty, we overcome God as once he was overcome by Jacob, who wrestled with him.

The image of the army shows that by his 'bride' not one individual is meant but the whole Church. The Church is 'terrible for God' through the irresistible power of the attraction it has for him. We advance victoriously towards God. God wishes one thing; we, in prayer, express another wish, and so we can be conquerors. The Bridegroom pleads with the Church, 'Turn away your eyes from me, for they have overcome me.' God declares himself defeated. We defeat him, with our doves' eyes.

In Exodus we read that God had decided to destroy Israel after it had sinned by making the golden calf. But Moses defeated that plan of God. He made him change his mind (Exodus 32). Every spiritual believer can do the same.

When the bride is with him, and he looks into her great pure, penetrating eyes, he lowers his own. The charm of her eyes is unbearable to him. The Bridegroom says, 'Your eyes have overcome me.' Rabbi ben Ezra translates this as, 'They are stronger than me.' The Septuagint renders it, 'They have caused me to flee.' Such can be our victory in prayer, through one loving look. Christians are called "more than conquerors". They are the conquerors of him who has overcome all.

When the apostles watched Jesus ascend into heaven, two angels came and stood by, and asked them, 'You men of Galilee, why stand you gazing up into heaven?' (Acts 1:10–11). If they had continued looking, perhaps Jesus would have been unable to separate himself from the earth. He could not have ascended. Their eyes would have impressed him so much that they would have persuaded him to fulfil their longing that he should remain with them.

We have God's command: 'Look unto me and be you saved, all the ends of the earth' (Isaiah 45:22). And in Solomon's Song we also have the command to the contrary: 'Turn away your eyes from me.' The latter verse serves as a warning to prying eyes, seeking out of curiosity to search mysteries which God has reserved only for himself.

The Bridegroom's words, 'Your teeth are as a flock of sheep . . . as a piece of pomegranate are your temples' are an almost verbatim repetition of the compliment which he pays the bride in chapter 4. Before she refused him access, he praised her. Now he pays her the same compliment, to show her that he has the same love for her after as before her fall. Even if his people are full of weakness, Jesus loves them. In the eyes of the king, the bride is as beautiful after her fall as she was on the day she was first presented to him. His love knows no alteration.

It is not necessary that the eyes of Christians be physically beautiful, for the bridegroom to be impressed. A Christian who has undergone torture is not a pretty sight.

A former Rumanian prisoner, R. Radina, describes his experiences in jail:

> Religious poems were being recited when, all at once, a man with his head red with blood entered the cell. Maddened with pain, he could not speak, but only howled like an animal. The prison director had beaten his face with a stone.
>
> An imprisoned Christian child, Mihica, was beaten with a stick on his head and on his lame leg. His crime was that he had shared his bread with other sufferers. He had considered a slice of bread too sumptuous a meal to eat all by himself.

In Cambodia, women were tortured with poisonous spiders. In Sarsar Sdam, children were torn to pieces and old women nailed to the doors before their houses were set on fire. Prisoners were hanged on trees after their bellies were ripped open.

Pure souls whose eyes are swollen, ringed with dark circles, bleeding, lift up a loving look to the Bridegroom. He has suffered for us as the Son of God, for whom goodness and love were the norms. These souls, though sinners, have loved him. Having to conquer their own nature in order to be able to love at all, when they look at him in adoration they are unconquerable. The prayers of martyrs are not rejected.

Radina also tells the story of the Rumanian Uniate priest, Onofrei Pompei. He was abused and hanged in the loft of his house. When the assassins departed the rope broke, and the priest came back to consciousness. God can save a person, even when it seems that all hope is gone. After that experience, Onofrei spent years in Communist prisons. Radina says of him, 'His expression radiated a strange light. He seemed a true saint.' This is the look which conquers even God.

His harem

The Bridegroom says, 'There are threescore queens, and fourscore concubines, and virgins without number. My dove, my undefiled, is but one; she is the only one of her mother, she is the choice one of she that bare her. The daughters saw her and blessed her; yes, the queens and the concubines, and they praised her' (6:8-9). Towards the end of his life Solomon had some 700 princesses as wives and 300 concubines. When he wrote the Song of Songs, they were fewer.

In the spiritual sense these words show us that all souls of believers are God's, that all the Christian churches are his. But we are not all equally loved. Only one is his dove, his undefiled, 'the only one of her mother'. There is one holy and apostolic Church, and it is made up of all the children of God. This Church is one, just as Noah's Ark in the period of the flood was one.

That does not mean, however, that those who are not members of it physically are excluded from the kingdom of God, or cannot be Jesus' sheep. There are some sheep which have to be brought into the true fold (John 10:16). The heart of Jesus embraces everybody in its love. But it is specially drawn to this choice dove, just as David, who had many wives, desired only Michal. Jesus longs for souls who belong to the only true Church with all their hearts.

In Communist lands, Jesus has his queens in every denomination. After eight years in prison I had grown accustomed to the routine. But one day a group of recently-arrested Orthodox priests were jailed. It was for them the very first day of the ordeal. It was winter; we sat on the bare concrete. From time to time, drunken guards would bawl 'All priests out!' The priests were taken from the cells and were severely beaten. I had known one of them for many years, and I asked him: 'Brother, are you grieved?' He answered, 'I know only of one grief, that of not being a saint.' In such circumstances, the words vividly showed the beauty of that soul, and made a lasting impression upon me.

Seventh-Day Adventists courageously stand up for their faith in Russia. Anatolii Miller, Karpenko Boris, Kovaltchuk and Galetskii are names of some of the Adventists who belong to Jesus and were jailed for their beliefs. The child, Michael Kozak, was kidnapped by the Communists from his parents, because they taught him the Adventist faith. When the child, who was interned in an atheistic boarding school, insisted on going back to his parents, he was put in a psychiatric asylum to be 'healed' of this desire. In spite of such things, the Adventists remain faithful to their Saviour.

In Cernanti in the Soviet Union, the Sedletztzy family received the sealed coffin of their son, who had refused to give up his faith while serving in the army. The officers demanded an immediate burial, but the family opened the coffin. They found the youth's face distorted from beatings, the eyes gouged out, the tongue torn out, the fingers cut off. He was a Baptist, faithful unto death.

In Rumania it seemed that St Basil the Great was alive again, because his words were on the lips of saints under interrogation. When a pastor was threatened with deportation, his reply was: 'Where can you exile me? I will be in my Father's world wherever you send me.'

To the threat of property confiscation, the reply was: 'That's all right by me, but you will need a very long ladder. I have gathered my treasures in heaven.'

'We will kill you!'

'We Christians do not fear death. It means passing over to a better life.'

'You are fools. We will not kill you, but keep you all in a prison cell behind locked doors and iron bars. We will not allow anybody to visit you.'

'We have a friend who can pass through locked doors and iron bars. We cannot be separated from the love of Christ.'

Christians are those who have promised faithfulness to God unto death. God keeps his promise. He never breaks it. Neither should we.

A Catholic seminarian, Ion Budu, died near me in a Communist prison. His greatest wish had been to be a missionary in India or Japan. His last words to we who were with him were these: 'If any of you ever go to Asia, tell the people there that I love them. May I die serving them through my longing for them, so that my death will be a sacrifice on their behalf.' I am the only survivor of that prison ward of dying men. When I went to Asia I saw how deeply moved the people were, as I told them how they had been loved for Christ's sake by a prisoner who had died a martyr death.

Jesus has many queens in every denomination, but also he has concubines. Concubines are girls or women who have illegitimate relationships with men. The only consistent attitude towards the Communist authorities is the Underground Church. The official churches, which have compromised with Communism, are anti-churches. Some of their pastors or bishops are real believers, but they are believers who waver between two masters, – Christ and Communism. They serve Communism, but stealthily slip away from it to say words of love to Christ. When he was on earth, too, Jesus had his secret believers. There are now secret believers in Christ among the members of the Communist Party, and even among the officers of the Communist Secret Police. However, they do not want to lose their livings and their positions. What they are doing is wrong, but Jesus accepts them as his concubines.

The glory of the Church

> Who is she that looks forth as the morning, fair as the moon, clear as the sun, and terrible as an army with banners?
>
> I went down to the garden of nuts to see the fruits of the valley, and to see whether the vine flourished, and the pomegranates budded.
>
> Before ever I was aware, my soul made me like the chariots of Ammi-nadib.
>
> Return, return, O Shulamite; return, return, that we may look upon you. What will you see in the Shulamite? As it were the company of two armies.
>
> (6:10–13)

The description of the Church in verse 6 is very like that in Revelation 12:1: 'A woman clothed with the sun, and the moon under her feet.' It is written in the *Zohar*:

> Israel's light will come little by little, until they will become strong. God will illumine them forever. All then will ask, 'Who is she that looks forth like the dawn,' this being a reference to the first tiny streak of the dawn; then 'Fair as the moon', the light of the moon being stronger than that of the dawn, and then 'clear as the sun', that is a still stronger light; and finally 'terrible as an army with banners', expressive of the light in its full strength.

> For, just as when the dawn emerges from darkness its light at first is faint, but gradually brightens until full daylight is reached, so when God bestirs Himself to shine upon the Community of Israel, He will first shed on them a streak of light like that of the daybreak which is still black, then increase it to make it 'fair as the moon', then 'clear as the sun', until it will be 'tremendous as an army with banners'.

She shines so intensely because she has followed Jesus' example. He has gone down (6:2). The bride too has gone down. Jesus said to Zaccheus, 'Make haste and come down.' Whoever belongs to Jesus must humble himself.

The bride says, 'I went down into the garden of nuts.' There she has learned something important! A believing soul is like a nut. It might be dirty and muddy outwardly, but the dirt never reaches the kernel. It is the same with the Christian when he is polluted by living in this world.

Because she has humbled herself and gone down, the Bridegroom takes her up, in the chariot of Ammi-nadib. Some commentators believe Aminadib to have been the name of one of Solomon's celebrated chariot drivers. The speed of his driving would be symbolic of the swift response of the Saviour to the call of love. But the old Jewish interpreters divided the world thus: *Ammi-nadib*. This means, 'the chariots of my willing, or princely, people.'

Return, O Shulamite

Seeing her thus glorified, the other girls call out to her. They shout what the average man, for centuries, has shouted to those who sit near to Jesus in his chariot of of trials: 'Return, return, O Shulamite; return, return!' The world is very demanding; it wants to draw us back to its own level.

At a jail in a Communist country, young officers would take girls out of the cells and invite them to go to restaurants with them. The girls, who had no fresh air in cells crammed with a hundred other unwashed people, were offered ice-cream and the cosy surroundings of a cinema, where they were shown erotic films. Most believers refused. One girl accepted. The Communists had been nice to her; she had to be nice too. The voice had been too insidious: 'Return, O Shulamite. Love me. You probably do not know the blessedness of the love of a man. I'll reveal it to you. My kisses will warm you.' She did not answer 'I belong to God', as she should have done. Everything else followed.

When she was freed, she accepted an invitation to speak to her fellow-inmates, attacking the faith. As she spoke against Jehovah, tears rolled down her face. She had returned to the world, while the others, the true brides, had remained steadfast.

Oleg Berdyuk, a Ukrainian writer in jail, has described how he came to accept the faith. He was a child when an artificial famine engineered by the Communists killed six million Ukrainians. He went to visit a relative, but she had starved to death. In an open Bible on her table, he read Magdalene's words, 'They have taken away my Lord, and I know not where they have laid him.' Turning round, she saw Jesus, who asked her, 'Woman, why do you weep?' The one she had considered dead was alive! (John 20:13–15).

That impressed him, but the Church disgusted him. Once he heard a priest chanting in the sanctuary, 'God, grant a long life to Stalin, God's chosen one, devout Christian and leader.' That was how religious stooges referred to the murderer of millions of innocents. This left him open to the call of the world: 'Return, O Shulamite.' He became an atheist.

But then he dreamed two dreams. In one, he saw Christ with an incredible weight on his shoulders, blood streaming down his body, his eyes sorrowful yet hopeful. In another dream, Christ, wearing a crown of thorns, showed him raging torrents, high mountains and cliffs, and said, 'Follow the path.' He asked, 'Why?' Christ replied only 'Go.'

Then one day he seemed to feel the presence of Christ while he was awake. It was not a thought about Christ. It was Christ himself. Oles knelt and said the only words that hallow God: 'I accept all that fate brings.' These words are similar to those of the virgin Mary: 'Be it unto me according to your word.'

And now, for the first time, we discover the name of the bride. It is 'Shulamite'; the Shulamite is the same person as the Shunamite. The bride's name is a reference to Abishag the Shunamite, one of David's concubines.

In Hebrew the word *shulamite* means 'peacemaker'. It is a name like *Solomon* which means 'peace'. The bride is a female Solomon. Jesus is the Prince of Peace (Isaiah 9), and the Church is the princess of peace, the Shulamite. Those who look at her can only think she is beautiful, accompanying angels in their dance.

The persecuted Church in truth 'looks forth as the morning' and is 'fair as the moon, clear as the sun'. The Orthodox monk Michael Ershov was in jail for forty-five years. While in prison he has healed many possessed, lame and blind people. What reason could have have for complaining or grumbling against Christianity? Instead of doing so, he used even his life in prison for doing good.

Kiwanukas, a trustee of the Jesus to the Communist World mission in Uganda, died in 1977. Together with fourteen other Christians, he was murdered by a hammer-blow to the head. His head was then cut off and taken to president Amin's house. His body was thrown into a lake.

Bishop Luwumba was asked by Amin whether he had any weapons. The Bishop showed him the Bible. Amin shot him first in the mouth, then in the chest. This murderer of Christians drank his blood and ate a piece of the victim's flesh. His advisers assisted him.

Despite such sufferings, the bride of Christ continues to spread the knowledge of his beauty in dark Uganda. She in truth looks forth as the morning and is fair as the moon, clear as the sun.

What a beautiful soul is the Russian believer Ghenadii Shimanov! Because he was an active believer who sought to win souls for Christ, he was put into a psychiatric asylum. There, Dr Shafran argued with him: 'Why won't you abandon your way of life, and hold on to your life, your freedom, and the happiness of your family? You could also keep the core of your faith intact. All you have to do is to give up propagating it. It only brings you sorrow. The odds are against you. You have the whole State opposed to you. In this sort of situation, every fight becomes an act of suicide. And what does your religion say about suicide? It forbids it. So, you see . . .

'One of my neighbours is a priest. We live in the same house. He is high in the Moscow patriarchy, an educated, intelligent man. One day he said to me, "Religion and life are two completely separate things which shouldn't be allowed to mix." A highly intelligent man! He can help you to reach decisions of which you are not capable on your own. Or do you prefer the martyr's crown?'

Shimanov replied briefly to the psychiatrist. 'The devil is smart.'

Shafran demanded, 'Am I the devil?'

'Oh, no. What ideas you have! I wasn't speaking about you. I am speaking about the devil. The real one.'

Shimanov refused to abandon his Christian activities. He remained in the asylum. He had to endure gagging and straightjackets. But he looked forth as the morning. He was fair as the moon, clear as the sun.

The end of verse 13 would be better translated, 'two companies of *mahanaim,*' a category of angels which specializes in sacred dancing. When God the king entered into his sanctuary, 'Singers went before, the players on instruments followed after; among them were the damsels playing with timbrels' (Psalm 68:24–25). So it happens when the Shulamite meets her Bridegroom. In Genesis 32:1–2 it is written, 'Jacob went on his way, and the angels of God met him. And when Jacob saw them, he said, "This is God's host": and he called the name of that place *Mahanaim*.'

≈ *Chapter 7* ≈

The holy dance

The Bridegroom says:

> 'How beautiful are your feet with shoes, O prince's daughter! the joints of your thighs are like jewels, the work of the hands of a cunning workman.
> Your navel is like a round goblet, which wants not liquor: your belly is like a heap of wheat set about with lilies.
> Your two breasts are like two young roes that are twins.
> Your neck is as a tower of ivory; your eyes like the fishpools in Heshbon, by the gate of Beth-rabbim: your nose is as the tower of Lebanon which looks toward Damascus.
> Your head upon you is like Carmel, and the hair of your head like purple; the king is held in the galleries.'
>
> (7:1–5)

The bride is here described as a dancer. People have always danced to the glory of their God. After they passed through the Red Sea, the Israelite women 'went out after [Miriam the prophetess] with timbrels and with dances' (Exodus 15:20). When David returned from his victory over Goliath, 'women came out of all the cities of Israel, singing and dancing, to meet King Saul' (1 Samuel 18:6). David danced mightily before God; Ecclesiastes says that there is a time to dance (Ecclesiastes 3:4). Jephthah's daughter came to meet him with timbrels and dances (Judges 11:34). Jeremiah prophesied that girls would rejoice with dancing when Jacob was ransomed. And when the prodigal son returned to his father, there was music and dancing.

The Shulamite also dances. She dances gracefully, like a true princess. Again her beauty is described to us, but with different imagery to that used before, because no earthly analogy alone is adequate to portray all the splendour of a faithful soul.

The description of the bride at this stage of her spiritual growth – after she has fallen into the sin of refusing to receive him – reveals her as more beautiful than she was immediately after the wedding. The sinner who repents is more beautiful in God's eyes than the righteous person; therefore the angels find greater joy in looking upon such a person.

One realizes, reading these verses, that the Bridegroom cannot find enough words to show his love to the bride who returns to him. He borrows images of oriental sensuality, and gives such free rein to his imagination that the translator is tempted to water down the vividness of the original. Solomon uses language which nobody in the West would dare to use, except to describe a woman abandoning herself totally, without reservation. It is the language which Solomon used to speak of the dancers in his harem. The Bridegroom praises even the most intimate charms of his bride. He praises her beauties, and she praises his. He honours us; we honour him.

His first word of praise is, 'How beautiful are your feet with shoes.' She has shod her feet with the preparation of the gospel of peace (Ephesians 6:15). Hers are the shoes of messengers bringing good news, telling of peace and salvation.

'The joints of your thighs are like jewels, the work of the hands of a cunning workman.' Saint Paul says that the Body of Christ – the Church – gets its nourishment by the joints (Colossians 2:19). This is an image of those pastors who lead their flocks well and teach them. Such pastors are jewels in the eyes of God.

The bride dances naked before the king, or wrapped in flimsy veils. Fascinated by her dance and her body, he exclaims, 'Your navel is like a round goblet, which wants not liquor; your belly is like a heap of wheat set about with lilies.' The belly is the organ from which food is distributed to the whole body. So it is also the secret castle, that which gives the bride a choice wine mixed with spices, which animates all her spiritual life. (The word translated as 'liquor' means in Hebrew 'mixture', indicating the variety of blessings she receives.)

Her two breasts are like 'two young roes that are twins'. This means that both Old and New Testaments are a delight to her.

Her neck is like 'a tower of ivory'. The neck, uniting the head and the body, is a symbol of faith. This means that her faith cannot be strangled.

Her nose is like the tower of Lebanon, one of the towers built by David in the north of Palestine to serve as an observation post against the Syrians.

It is important that believers have a keen sense of smell. They must discern the spirits. As from the tower of Lebanon one could see enemy armies from afar, so the bride scents heresy which is far off.

Our intellect prefers to see the similarities between doctrines rather than the differences between them. Consequently it gives vague information. We need a nose like the bride's, capable of discerning the spirits. Pastors in the Underground Church need such a nose to discover Communist infiltrators.

The tower looks towards Damascus, the capital of Syria, always Israel's enemy. To her enemies she is 'terrible as an army with banners'.

Her head is 'like Carmel', a hill full of rich vegetation. She has a beautiful abundance of red hair. The Nazirites were a kind of monk living at that time. No razor ever passed over their heads. It was believed that the secret of their power lay in their hair. The bride's power of attraction also resides in the richness of her hair, those locks that bind the King of Kings.

There are not enough words to describe the beauty of the bride of Christ under persecution today. In Guinea in Africa, under the dictator Sekou Toure, Cardinal Tchidimbo and other Christians were kept for up to eight days without food or water in the tropical heat, in cells full of rats, lice and insects. The cables which bound them cut into their flesh. They were flogged and called 'Christian dirt'. Three hundred prisoners were locked into a single unventilated room, where they suffocated.

Others were given electric shocks while their hands were tied to iron bars placed so high that only the tips of their toes reached the floor. For days the full weight of their bodies was taken by their tied hands.

Some were forced to kneel on sharp stones. Their skin was flayed and pepper was poured on their open wounds. Hot pepper was introduced into the rectum; this is a torture which produces unspeakable pain. All the time they were told, 'If you denounce others, we will give you water.'

Some died; they did not become Judases. The Cardinal survived, and, after his release, he wrote in Rome a splendid book demonstrating how suffering has purified him and made him love the Bridegroom more.

In South Africa, the Communist-backed terrorists, supported by the leftist World Council of Churches, hacked pregnant women to death. They slit the throats of babies. They peeled the skin from an old man's face, and left him to die in the blazing sun, impaled on a barbed-wire fence. They cut off lips. They gouged out eyes. But the bride of Christ in South Africa remains unafraid.

One of the strangest verses in the whole book follows the praise of the bride: 'The king is held in the galleries.' The Hebrew word translated as 'held' is *asar* which also means 'imprisoned with chains and fetters'. The word *rahat* which the Authorized Version here renders as 'gallery' is in Genesis 30 translated as 'gutters'.

All Jewish commentators agree that the king spoken of here is the Messiah. The *Kabbalah* says that he does not come yet, because God keeps him bound in heaven in golden chains. Others believe that he is bound there with locks of women's hair, which are like eddies of water in water troughs. Hence this image. He ardently wishes to come, but God restrains him in this way.

We cannot accept these fancies. The Messiah *has* come. Jesus is his name. The explanation of the verse is much simpler than those above. The king has found himself a bride in the world's gutter. Publicans, crooks, loose women, murderers, those of us with more 'respectable' sins – all of us are lost. When we are converted he admires the beauties of our souls, described in detail in the preceding verses. His love for his bride binds him to her as if with fetters.

Jesus admires his bride

The Bridegroom says:

'How fair and how pleasant are you, O love, for delights!
  This your stature is like to a palm tree, and your breasts to clusters of grapes.
  I said, I will go up to the palm tree, I will take hold of the boughs thereof: now also your breasts shall be as clusters of the vine, and the smell of your nose like apples.
  And the roof of your mouth like the best wine for my beloved, that goes down sweetly, causing the lips of those that are asleep to speak.'

(7:6–9)

There will never be anything more delightful than love which bears all things, believes all things and hopes and endures all; love which is extended even to enemies and beyond the grave; love which gives its life for the beloved.

Love is the wisest thing. That is why the Syriac translation calls this book, *The Wisdom of the Wise*.

Jesus speaks to the bride in the language of admiration. We must not be surprised at this. Faithfulness was a part of Jesus' nature. For him it was natural to be faithful. He came from heaven. But faithfulness is practised also by many downtrodden, wronged men of this earth, who do not understand the reason for their suffering. They still maintain their faithful, pure love for God, and that is something for which God himself has admiration.

I knew a railway worker who was a Christian. His only daughter, whom he loved very much, died when she was fourteen. She was drowned head-downwards in a ditch full of sewage. The man did not torment himself with doubts, but continued in his love for God, and was prepared to suffer imprisonment for his sake. God made our souls pleasant and beautiful, and he admires us as an artist admires his work.

The stature of the bride is like that of a palm tree – straight, powerful, high and gracious. The palm tree was an emblem of Israel. A medal was struck for the Roman Emperor Titus, who destroyed the Jewish state. It bore the figure of a grieving woman seated beneath a palm tree. The inscription read, *Judaea capta* – 'Judaea is taken'. She might be a captive, but Israel was still a palm tree, standing erect, refusing to bow to heathen idolatry.

The Bridegroom says to himself, 'I will go up to the palm tree, I will take hold of the boughs thereof.' He is expressing his desire to be strongly united with the believing soul. Let us take heed of the words 'I will go up'. There are believers towards whom Jesus 'goes up'. He said that there are some who will do greater works than his (John 14:12). Towards those disciples, he ascends. He will grasp the boughs of these palm trees. When he does so, it will be seen whether they are strong and resistant or not. A palm tree which he embraces becomes sanctified.

Not only in Solomon's temple, but also in Ezekiel's ideal temple, there were figures of palm trees as well as cherubim.

The use of the palm tree as a symbol for a bride is emphasized by the Hebrew text in these passages, since the word used for 'palm tree' is not the usual *tamar*, but its female form, *timmorah*.

The bride's breasts 'shall be as clusters of the vine'. Just as grapes refresh a man, so Jesus is refreshed by our fruitfulness, by our work for him. One of the characteristics of oriental love is that it takes pleasure in anticipating its joys beforehand. So Jesus exults beforehand, in the joy which he will receive from faithful souls.

In the entire Soviet Republic of Moldavia, there were only two Catholic churches. One of them, in Sloboda-Rashkovo, was bulldozed to the ground by the police. They are mindless. They destroyed the physical building, yet the church is now more beautiful than it was before.

The Catholics, weeping, lifted from the mud the church's Communion wafers, which they believed to be the real body of Christ. They ate them with reverence. Walls had been torn down, but the Christians' reverence for God had increased. Jesus 'goes up' toward such believers.

In the Soviet Union the police frequently raid meetings of the Baptist Underground Church, confiscating Bibles, hymnbooks, and the private purses of some of the believers. They kick Christians in the belly and in the chests. The Communists are mad. Usually the believers, while they are being beaten, pray and sing. Such music has a spiritual beauty of its own. To these believers, Jesus says, 'How fair and pleasant are you, O love, for delights!' These are the Christians likened by him to palm trees, to whom he goes up.

The Communists do not know the words of Gregory of Palama: 'The Christian's life is outside, beyond, and higher than its physical self.' 'Truth', wrote Luther, 'becomes more triumphant when attacked, more glorious when oppressed.'

'Come, my beloved'

The bride says: 'Come, my beloved, let us go forth into the field; let us lodge in the villages. Let us go up early to the vineyards; let us see if the vines flourish, whether the tender grapes appear, and the pomegranates bud forth: there I will give you my loves' (7:11–12).

We are the object of two desires. God says to Cain, 'Sin lies at the door. And its desire is for you' (Genesis 4:7). In Psalm 45 it is written, 'Harken, O daughter, and consider, and incline your ear; forget also your own people, and your father's house; so shall the king greatly desire your beauty' (Psalm 45:10–11). Two powers compete for our love.

And now she who has chosen Jesus will demonstrate how greatly she desires him. She says, 'Come, my beloved, let us go forth into the field; let us lodge in the villages.' Faithful souls hate towns full of sin and noise. It is difficult to serve the Lord if things continually distract you. Isaac went out into the field to meditate quietly (Genesis 24:63). Jesus advises us, 'When you pray, enter into your closet, and when you have shut your door, pray to your Father' (Matthew 6:6). The bride does not seek amusement in noisy places. She desires solitude. She doesn't want Jesus to judge the Church with the same judgement that will be meted out to the spoilt residents of the town. Jesus will see the reality of her faith in a quiet, rural environment. In company with him, she will go early to the vineyard to see if the vines are flourishing and whether the tender grapes have appeared. They will examine souls, to see whether they have grown in grace and truthfulness.

Wang-Min-Dao, a hero of the faith in China, broke under torture and acknowledged before a large crowd, 'I am an anti-revolutionary criminal. I am grateful to the government for pardoning me and saving me from the depths of my sins.' But he repented later. He went to the police station with his wife and said, 'I am a Judas. I have betrayed my Lord. Imprison me.' He sat in jail for over twenty years. Now he is free in Red China.

If the Bridegroom and the bride go up to the vineyards of Red China, they will find that the vine has flourished, and the tender grape has appeared.

In Omsk, in Russia, the Baptist Church was celebrating Easter. Its members had gathered at the home of Sister Helen Siusa. Thirty policemen, mostly drunk, rushed in and jumped upon the believers. They ruthlessly beat up everybody, including old people, women and children.

When the police tried to arrest the preachers, men who had already been in prison, the children cried, 'We will not give up our fathers!' Their tears were heartrending, but the police did not think so. They kicked them with their boots and shouted: 'You are enemies of the people! You should have no work and no food! There is no law to protect you!'

The Christians, however, were unafraid. That same afternoon they held their worship service again in the same house.

A Russian Pentecostal believer, Vashtshenko, had been twice in prison. His four sons carried on his work. One of them, Hariton, became a Pentecostal bishop. His children were asked to deny Christ and to blaspheme in school. They refused to comply. They were taken away from their parents and put into an atheistic boarding school. Their mother was forbidden to visit them. This is what they wrote to their parents: 'We weep at night. The boys beat us. But do not worry, Papa and Mama, for God is our protection. We weep because we are not allowed to come home.'

Their daughter, Valia, refused to eat without saying grace. She was mocked but with other Christian children, she continued to thank God for her food. She wrote: 'The director shouts at us and this is good; the bigger our sorrow, the nearer we are to God. By God's will I shall remain a believer. I do not want to learn anything in this atheistic school.'

An Orthodox priest, Talantov, and his son were killed by the Communists. His other son, Boris, continued to witness openly for Christ. For this he also was put into prison, where he died.

The Baptist preacher Peter Vins died in prison for his faith. His wife too was in prison for three years. Their son George, General Secretary of the Baptist Union of the USSR, also went to jail.

The bride can quietly call the heavenly Bridegroom to get up early to go with her to the vineyard. They will see the vine flourish and the tender grapes appear. Christianity in Communist countries bears rich fruit for God.

A pleasant perfume

The bride says, 'The mandrakes give a smell, and at our gates are all manner of pleasant fruits, new and old, which I have laid up for you, O beloved' (7:13).

The precise identification of the mandrake is unknown. It could be the cantaloupe. This has a pleasant perfume, which typifies the perfume spread in this world by believers; especially by young believers who have been born into a family of the faithful and have not known the life of sin.

In antiquity the fruit and roots of the mandrake were thought to have aphrodisiac qualities. Leah gave mandrake to Rachel. The fragrance we spread in the world stimulates the faculty of love in others.

Unlike the evil workers in the vineyard who have withheld their harvest from the master, the bride has laid up fruits at the gate. He is not greedy; he is not in a hurry to collect them; he allows them to mature.

We know how to keep the fruits which were not picked by the master, just as women know how to preserve fruit. The bride has kept new and old fruit for her master. 'Every scribe who is instructed unto the kingdom of heaven is like unto a man that is a householder, who brings forth out of his treasure things new and old' (Matthew 13:52)

≈ *Chapter 8* ≈

'If you were my brother'

The bride says:

'O that you were as my brother, that sucked the breasts of my mother! When I should find you without, I would kiss you; yes, I should not be despised.

I would lead you, and bring you into my mother's house, who would instruct me: I would cause you to drink of spiced wine of the juice of my pomegranate.

His left hand should be under my head, and his right hand should embrace me.

I charge you, O daughters of Jerusalem, that you stir not up, nor awake my love, until he please.

Who is this that comes up from the wilderness, leaning upon her beloved?

I raised you up under the apple tree: there your mother brought you forth: there she brought you forth that bore you.

Set me as a seal upon your heart, as a seal upon your arm: for love is strong as death; jealousy is cruel as the grave: the coals thereof are coals of fire, which has a most vehement flame.

Many waters cannot quench love, neither can the floods drown it: if a man would give all the substance of his house for love, it would be utterly condemned.'

(8:1–7)

The most intimate of relationships with Jesus cannot be expressed in public. Before the world, we may only have the relationship between brother and sister, in which kisses are considered respectable.

The Shulamite is modest. She knows how far she is from what a wife should be. She still has to learn. So, she says that if she should find him, she would lead him into her mother's house, the Church.

What daring words she uses! We are accustomed to think he leads us as king, shepherd and teacher. But we can also lead him – by prevailing love and prevailing prayer. In fact a contest is taking place. He wishes to lead us to the mansions he has prepared for us in his Father's house: we insist on first taking him to the house of our mother (we shall speak further of this). There, the bride will learn to give him spiced wine, the juice of her pomegranate. The mother, the Church, has long experience of the kind of adoration which pleases him. We all have to learn from her.

The bride's friends ask, 'Who is this that comes up from the wilderness leaning upon her beloved?' First it was the Jewish people. Now, it is the Church and every individual believing soul. Every 'coming out' from the wilderness is a 'coming up'.

The wilderness is exhausting. You cannot come out of it in your own strength, but only by leaning upon the Beloved. The literal translation is, 'her arm under his arm-pit' – an expression of great familiarity.

She says, 'I raised you up under the apple tree.' We believers raise up the Saviour through our prayer. The disciples woke him up repeatedly during a storm: 'Awake! why do you sleep? Awake!' This is also the frequent prayer of the Psalmist.

She prays that she might keep his love: 'Set me as a jewel upon your heart, as a seal upon your arm.' Men in the Orient sometimes wear, on their breast or on their arm, jewels with the portrait or the name of their bride engraved on them. She wants the Beloved to have such a jewel. She would like to be a seal on his heart, so that nothing else might enter. The soul wants to know for certain that it will remain in God's love.

The bride's prayer has been fulfilled. John's Gospel tells us that Jesus said on the Cross the word which is rendered in Greek as *tetelestai* – 'It is finished.' In the New Testament all Jesus' words are translated, for he spoke in Aramaic. The word he must have actually used is *kalah*. It has two meanings. One is 'It has been accomplished' or 'finished'. The other is, 'bride'. It is possible that his very last word before death was a loving sigh for his bride.

Of some souls God has said, 'I have engraved you upon my hand.' God says to a believer who has reached this spiritual state, as he said to Zerubbabel, 'I will take you O Zerubbabel and will make you as a signet; for I have chosen you' (Haggai 2:23). But before this is fulfilled, terrible things must happen.

What God says to Zerubbabel is: 'I will overthrow the throne of kingdoms, and I will destroy the strength of the kingdoms of the heathen; and I will overthrow the chariots, and those that ride in them; and the horses and their riders shall come down, every one by the sword of his brother. In that day . . . will I take you . . . as a seal (the same word as is translated 'seal' in Haggai 2:22–23).

Sometimes we pray foolishly. We are like doctors who would like to destroy tuberculosis but object to the destruction of the microbes that cause it. We want the kingdom of God, the only state in which we will know in perfection what it is like to be near the Beloved; but as often as something happens that signals the destruction of Satan's kingdom, we make intercession: 'Don't let anything be destroyed!' The churches storm heaven with their prayers.

That is what I alluded to when I compared the desire of the Bridegroom, who wants to lead us into his Father's mansions, to that of the bride, who wants to lead him to her mother's house. We will come to be a seal on his heart only when our prayers quieten down, to 'Hallowed be thy name, thy kingdom come, thy will be done' – though I know that this will involve the perishing of all those who, despite having had a better light offered to them, oppose it.

Even when you have arrived at this place, vigilance is necessary. The assurance that one is in the favour of God can only be maintained by patience, goodness and righteousness.

Love is like death

Now the bride brings arguments to show why she has such pretensions, and why she makes such demands.

Death and love have many common features. Just as nothing can resist death or avoid it, and in the end everything must come under the law of death, so it is with love. He whom death assails, must die; he whom love assails, must love. The phenomenon of death makes man understand that there are limits to human power.

However, I cannot resist telling a joke in this context. A pastor was once delivering a thundering sermon about sin and hell. 'One thing is certain!' he said. 'Every man, woman and child in this parish will die one day. There is no escape!'

A boy in the front seat began to laugh.

'Every person in the parish will one day die!' the pastor reiterated.

The boy continued to laugh.

'What are you laughing at?' demanded the pastor angrily.

'I'm not from this parish!' said the boy.

Death happens of necessity. There is no point in dissipating energy in struggling against it. It can be postponed for a time, but not escaped. So with love. You cannot decide with whom you will fall in love. There are two people destined for each other: when they meet, the barriers fall. Because of love, Edward VIII of Britain gave up the throne of an empire, for a divorced woman; King Charles II of Rumania did the same. The elect bride can do no other than love Jesus ardently. He can do no other than love her.

It seems at first glance strange that the bride could not have found more appropriate images of love than death and the grave. The *Zohar* asks the question whether God's words when he finishes the creation – 'And behold, it was very good' (Genesis 1:31) – included in their meaning the Angel of Death. The *Zohar* concludes:

Concerning this mystery, R. Simeon gave us the following explanation: 'And behold it was good' refers to the Angel of Life; 'very' to the Angel of Death, for he is of greater importance. And why? When the Holy One, blessed be He, created the world, all was prepared for the coming of man, who is the king of this world. Man was fashioned to walk in the straight way, as it is written: 'God has made man upright, but they have sought out many inventions' (Ecclesiastes 7:29). He made man upright, but he gave himself over to corruption and was therefore driven out of the Garden of Eden. This garden was planted by the Holy One, blessed be He, on the earth, and made an exact likeness of its prototype, the Paradise above, and all supernal forms were fashioned and shaped in it, and the cherubs were there – not those carved in gold or any material that could be fashioned by human hands, but of supernal light, fashioned and broidered through the agency of the perfect Name of the Holy One. All the images and forms of all things in this world were there fashioned, all having the similitude of the things in this world. And this place is the abode of holy spirits, both of those that have come into this world, and also of those that have not yet come into this world.

Those that are about to come are invested with garments and with faces and bodies like those in this world, and they gaze upon the glory of their Lord until the time comes for them to appear in the world. When they leave the Garden for that purpose, these spirits put off their celestial bodies and garments and take on the bodies and garments of this world; they henceforth make their abode in this world in the garments and bodies fashioned from the seed of procreation. So when the time comes for the spirit to leave this world again, it cannot do so until the Angel of Death has taken off the garment of this body. When that has been done, he again puts on that other garment in the Garden of Eden of which he had had to divest himself when he entered this world. And the whole joy of the spirit is in that celestial body. In it he rests and moves, and contemplates continually the supernatural mysteries which, when he was in the earthly body, he could neither grasp nor understand. When the soul clothes herself with the garments of that world, what delights, what joys, she experiences! And who caused the body to be inhabited by the spirit? Why, he who took off the garment of flesh, the Angel of Death!

The bride sees nothing wrong in death, which brings her into his embrace. For her, it is natural to compare love to death.

In the fourth century AD, in Sebaste in Armenia, forty young Christians were sentenced to death by freezing. In winter they were forced to go naked into a river. They were told that if they denied their faith, they would be allowed to come out and warm themselves at a fire that was ready on the shore. The mother of one of them helped her son to enter the vehicle in which they were to be taken to the river. She did not weep, but said, 'Go, walk with your brethren. Don't linger. Do not arrive in the Lord's presence after them.'

One of them did recant. But then a soldier watching on

the shore saw an angel descend from heaven, with forty crowns in his hand. He placed a crown on every head, but was left with one over; the youth for whom it was intended had fled the Angel of Death, the harbinger of the final triumph.

The soldier immediately stripped off his clothes and plunged into the cold water, shouting, 'I am coming, Angel!' He died with the rest. That is how brides feel and act.

Just as death is impressed by nothing, and cannot be bribed or persuaded not to act, so is love. Love for God, just like death, takes away from man the desire for transitory things. Just as death never releases its prey, neither does love.

Surely, this is what the love of God towards us is like. For his beloved bride, he puts aside his glory, his righteousness, his law, his divinity, his eternity. For her he becomes a slave. He dies on a cross – for her. His love is a love to the end.

His jealousy is cruel as the grave. It is love's legitimate reaction against any insults brought to it by the beloved. He is jealous when we fall into idolatry. We, for our part, have to be jealous and intolerant of the things that belong to our lower nature. Our prayer is, 'Lord, be jealous of me; and do not give me into the hand of anything else.'

A book without the word 'God'

The bride says, 'The coals [of jealousy] are coals of fire, which has a most vehement flame.' The Authorized Version here translates exactly what is in the Masoretic Hebrew text. However, some Jewish copyists wondered how it was that this biblical book contains no mention of

God. Therefore, in some manuscripts they divided the last word of this verse, *shalhebetiah* ('vehement flame'), into *shalhebet-Jah* – 'flame of the Lord' (*Jah* being the older form of *Jehovah*). The same is found in several English translations.

This is acceptable but superfluous. God resonates in every verse in this book. God is love. Where bride and Bridegroom show burning, loyal feelings towards each other, when you have said 'love' you have said 'God'. In this Song, mutual love and the giving of self to each other, and to the One to whom they less directly belong, is religion itself. There is no need to dress it up with religious phraseology. Solomon's Song does not include the word 'God'. But it is an eloquent proof of his existence.

The philosopher, Immanuel Kant, said that the moral law demands that men be rewarded in proportion to their virtues. Since in everyday life evil men often fare better than those who are good, it follows that there must be another existence, and there must be a God who gives rewards in eternity. Brides like the one in Solomon's Song surely do not get their rewards on earth.

Vincent Van Gogh was a preacher in a squalid mining village in Belgium. He became more humble than the humble, and renounced everything: house, clothes and food. He overwhelmed his hearers with his evangelical fervour. During a typhoid epidemic he gave away as bandages even the few rags that he wore. Then he discovered his talent for painting. Now, over ninety years later, his paintings sell for millions. But Van Gogh himself never made any money from his art. He continued to live in the darkest misery, creating master-works.

Chinese Christians have always endured suffering with fortitude. During the Boxer Rebellion, when killers entered the house of sister Ming, she asked them to allow her the favour of changing her dress. She then put on her bridal gown and most beautiful ornaments. For her, death was a wedding feast. And so she died.

Prisoners brought to the Wronski jail in Poland were asked, 'Who among you is a believing Christian?' All stepped forward.

'We have kneeling chairs for you,' they were told.

The prisoners were then made to kneel on ordinary stools. 'Pray aloud!' they were ordered. 'And take your shoes off!' During their prayers, blows fell on their bare feet. The Christians all had difficulty walking next day.

In Wronski, the cells are cold. Many windows are broken. Christmas dinner consisted of plain bread and overcooked potatoes, yet the prisoners had to work at felling trees. Whoever stayed in the toilet more than five minutes received truncheon blows.

'Many waters cannot quench love, neither can the floods drown it.' God, loving the little Israel, did not forsake it for the cause of some mighty empire. On the contrary, he gave other nations as a ransom for Israel. The love of God for the faithful soul will last forever. This is the summary of this whole book, and its moral. The love magnified in this book is true love, which does not lose heart when faced with great danger. It is a love which inspires courage and sacrifice, preferring voluntary poverty to servile richness; a love which hates with vigour everything which is false and mean; a love which matures into calmness and faithfulness.

Priceless love

'If a man would give the substance of his house for love, it would utterly be condemned.' Such love is not for sale. Like wisdom, it cannot be bartered for gold. It cannot be bought with silver.

It is written in the Bible, 'Buy truth.' (Proverbs 23.23) Jesus said, 'I counsel you to buy of me gold tried in the fire, that you may be rich; and white raiment, that you may be clothed' (Revelation 3:18). Interpreting words like these, upon which he had not meditated very profoundly, Simon the sorcerer offered money to the apostles, and said to them, 'Give me also this power, that on whomsoever I lay hands, he may receive the Holy Ghost' (Acts 8;19). His fault was that he did not understand spiritual things. God's gifts cannot be bought with money. Isaiah says, 'Buy wine and milk without money and without price' (Isaiah 55:1).

The commandment is strict: it is forbidden to pay for God's gifts with money.

To simply give everything is the responsibility of all Christians. Simon sinned by the fact that he still had money, and he offered it to the disciples in exchange for something. The first Christians gave everything at the time of their conversion.

The gifts of God *can* be bought, but it is through the renunciation of sin and vanity. Moreover, riches are incompatible with love; the believer must consistently refuse the hope of riches. As Jesus refuses our money and seeks us, so the bride must seek not his gifts, but Jesus himself.

A missionary, captured by the Chinese Communists some years ago, was about to be beheaded. Suddenly she began to laugh. Her captors asked, 'What is so funny about being beheaded?'

'I was just thinking,' she replied, 'how ridiculous my head would look rolling down the hill!' They let her go. With this sister, love was as strong as death.

After the Russian Revolution a civil war raged for many years between the conservative population and their foes, the Communists. At that time an Orthodox priest, walking down the street, saw five soldiers of the conservative White Army tie a Communist soldier to a tree and prepare to execute him. On seeing the priest, the officer who led the firing squad greeted him with the usual Russian greeting, 'Bless us, father.'

'I can't bless a killing,' answered the priest.

Moved, the officers freed their prisoner.

A few weeks later a woman called that priest to administer the last rites to her dying son. As he entered the house, the priest heard the son yell to his mother, 'Why did you call a priest? All those villains must be killed! I am a Communist. I can't stand priests.'

But then, recognizing the priest, he exclaimed, 'You are the one who saved me from being shot. You said, "I can't bless a killing." Do you see the big knife on the table? My assignment was to kill you with it. If you had known that, would you still have stopped my execution?'

'Even in that case,' replied the priest, 'I would not have blessed the killing, because God has forgiving love for us all. God has sent me a second time to save you.'

A minute later, the man was dead, but all the hatred had disappeared from his face. The love of that priest was also stronger than death.

In the Soviet Union, there still are brothers and sisters in psychiatric asylums. A letter smuggled out told of Sitchovka, a prisoner in an asylum, who was shown a straitjacket by a Secret Police officer posing as a doctor. He said, 'Don't worry – we won't use it on you. We've got something better; the chemical straitjacket.'

The prisoner was led into a room where cats, under the influence of an alkaloid drug, were unable to move even when threatened, pinched or when a flame was brought near their whiskers. When an officer tried to push a cat forward, it displayed every sign of stupor. Another cat stood motionless, with its hind legs on a chair and its front legs on the floor. In the room were cats, mice, apes and birds, all drugged by some poison, standing petrified like statues.

The officer laughingly said to the believer, 'One of your brethren mentioned the prophecy that when Jesus returns, wolves will dwell with lambs. We don't need Jesus. We do it ourselves! We have our own saviour, and we will break you with it. You can't withstand this.'

Our Christian brother added in his letter, 'The magicians at Pharaoh's court also imitated the miracles that Moses did. But Moses remained God's man.'

The love of such Christians, who know these horrors await them if they remain faithful and who continue to serve the Church, is not only as strong as death but stronger still. It is stronger than the fear of being deprived of your mind for ever.

A little sister

The bride says:

> 'We have a little sister, and she has no breasts; what shall we do for our sister in the day when she will be spoken for?
>
> If she be a wall, we will build upon her a palace of silver: and if she be a door, we will enclose her with boards of cedar.
>
> I am a wall, and my breasts are like towers; then was I in his eyes as one that found favour.'
>
> (8:8–10)

Here we have a supplement to the Song of Songs. Once she is sure of the unlimited love of God, the bride has her mind at rest and can turn to the problem of her sister. Jesus and the bride, united in full reciprocal love, discuss what is to be done with the younger sister who has no breasts yet, which means that she has no prominent qualities in her body; she has done no exceptional deeds in the service of God.

Jesus assures the bride that the Holy Trinity will do

everything for her. If she be a wall – which means, if she is a person who cannot fall under temptation, if she is strong as iron, if she can resist – then God will do her great honour. But if she is a door, which can easily be opened – if she falls easily in sin, if her virtue is not solid – she will be enclosed with walls of cedar, a strong and durable wood. The weak believer is guarded in a special way, though even believers who are able to resist sin are not left unwatched, because strong castles can also fall.

The bride is assured of what God will do for her small sister, remembering the miracles he did for her who is like a wall and who has breasts like twin roes, typifying unconquerable virtues. She has found favour with him. The Shulamite, the princess of peace, has found *shalom* (peace) with Solomon, the Prince of Peace.

Some Christians are strong. All seductions rebound off them. On such strong walls, Jesus can build castles of silver. I am reminded of Hannington, the Anglican bishop of Uganda, who was eaten by cannibals. He went to his death reciting the Lord's words, 'Love your enemies, bless them that curse you.' On that wall, God built a splendid castle. Hannington's sons became missionaries and baptized their father's murderers. Those converted cannibals told the story.

Some twenty Russian girls were novices in a secret convent. When it was discovered, they were all sent to Siberia. The last advice of the abbess to the girls was to stay together if possible, and to say as soon as they met anybody – be it friend or enemy, policeman or fellow-prisoner – that they belonged to Christ.

They were sent to forced labour, and had to fell trees. One night, a group of other prisoners who were common criminals came to the girls' barracks. The girls were frightened, but the men told them, 'You have spoken about your faith. So, explain to us about God. We have not seen a priest for thirty years. We need a word from God.' From that night the barracks became a mission centre.

Even the guards sympathized. Many people were converted, and the novices baptized them. The former criminals helped the girls fulfil their work quotas so that they could have time for prayer.

These are the brides of Christ, with great and strong breasts.

Solomon's vineyard

The bride says:

'Solomon had a vineyard at Baalhamon; he let out the vineyard unto keepers; every one for the fruit thereof was to bring a thousand pieces of silver.

My vineyard, which is mine, is before me: you, O Solomon, must have a thousand, and those that keep the fruit thereof two hundred.

You who dwell in the gardens, the companions hearken to your voice: cause me to hear it.

Make haste, my beloved, and be like to a roe or to a young hart upon the mountains of spices.'

(8:11–14)

In Hebrew *hamon* means 'a great, noisy crowd'. Solomon had a vineyard in Baalhamon. Jesus has his vineyard, his Church, in the midst of a noisy multitude.

The bride discusses with him what fruit their vineyards must produce. She says to him, 'My vineyard, which is mine, is before me.' Before, she did not look after her vineyard. Now she has decided to care for it, so that God will be able to build a palace of silver upon her testimony. She promises Solomon one thousand pieces of silver from the profits of her vineyard, and allows two hundred for the workers who tend it.

The *Zohar* rightly says, 'Wherever the name of Solomon is mentioned in Solomon's Song it is holy, except in the words "A thousand unto you, O Solomon." ' The author has descended from celestial heights down to financial dealing. He could not help revealing that the Word of God has passed through human hands.

Rembrandt painted a splendid picture of the good Samaritan. In front of the inn where the wounded man was brought, he painted a dog relieving itself. This is the most prosaic thing in life. In the middle of his most tragic tirade, Shakespeare's King Lear speaks to the Fool in bawdy language. No work of art or religion is exempted from at least a token acknowledgement of the meanness of human nature.

But there is also an important lesson in this verse. The bulk of a church's finances must go towards the propagation of the gospel. Ministers must be provided for, but not luxuriously. It is a scandal that some ministers in the USA have large salaries, when those in the Third World often live at poverty level. And as for those under Communist persecution, who thinks of them?

Now it is time for the Bridegroom to depart. He goes into the mountains: the bride remains in the gardens below. His last words are, 'You who dwell in the gardens, the companions [the angels, the glorified saints] hearken to your voice: cause me to hear it.' He asks her to pray. Thus this beautiful book comes to an end.

Towards the close of his life, Solomon was disappointed in the Shulamite to whom he had dedicated his Song. In the beginning her love was passionate, but it finished with who knows what tragedy. When he was old, the king wrote, 'I did not find a woman.' Will our soul also disappoint the Prince of Peace? When the Son of Man comes, will he find faith on earth?

The bride's love is great, but great love needs to be tended to remain great. If you put a single gram of radium in a vault and leave it untouched, after a certain period it will only be half a gram of radium and after a further period it will only be one quarter of a gram. Radium disintegrates. Love disintegrates, too. It must be kept warm, and must be made to grow through frequent meditation and contemplation of the Beloved. The love described in the Song of Solomon, where the bride gives the Bridegroom a thousand pieces of silver, is not a hopeless ideal. It really exists.

Igor Ogurtsov, an Orthodox believer, was sentenced to twenty years in prison for his Christian activities. Converted by his grandmother, he was one of the organizers of the Social Christian Union for the Liberation of the Russian People. For a time he had been detained in a psychiatric asylum, for being too religious.

A fellow-prisoner describes him as a man of pathos. All who drew near him felt that Ogurtsov was far ahead of his contemporaries. He declared that his aim was the Christianization of politics, economics and culture. After ten years of prison and torture, he was still strong enough to write:

> There is only one choice before mankind: a free return to God and acceptance of His love, whereupon all the powers and beauty of man will flourish; or departure from God, whereupon we will have a Satanocracy and a twisted conscience, as a result of losing the true aim and purpose of life. Capitalism and its sick child, Communism, can be conquered only by the Christianization of the whole social order.

At forty he had lost all his teeth in jail. He suffered from avitaminosis and hypertonicity. He could hardly stand on his feet, but he still had to do slave labour. Neither the world nor the churches mention him, but he offered a great feast to Christ. He paid to him his full due: a thousand pieces of silver.

Petras Plumpa, a Catholic, is serving a five-year sentence. He writes from prison:

Wherever we live, the most important problem is the salvation of souls. If the King of souls has sown us in the field of sorrows, let us bloom in sorrow; if in solitude, then in solitude let us bloom. The Creator sows the most beautiful flowers in inaccessible places among mountain tracts, and, though no man sees them, they have their own value. The anguish of a soul, though unseen, can be plucked and offered like a flower to the Saviour. This is the most beautiful decoration in the altar of Jesus. Lacking such decoration, even the finest churches have sad faces.

For the sake of souls like this, our Beloved, who is now like a roe or a young hart upon the mountains of spices, will return. The bride who dwells in the garden of faith amidst sorrows waits for him.

≈ *Last Considerations* ≈

Arriving at the end of this book, we wonder. Everything written in it, even the most intimate sexual details, is about the love of a faithful soul for a Bridegroom she has never seen. She speaks of kisses, of caresses, of embraces, although she has never touched him, nor even perceived him with her senses.

It is so. But in a similar way, our universe is mostly hydrogen, and no-one has ever seen a hydrogen atom. Millions of them would fit on a pinhead. The hydrogen atom is a speculation in our minds. Yet the whole of our physics and chemistry is based on unseen atoms. We can even construct atomic bombs, using atoms which we cannot see. Space and time are only mental constructs. But that does not stop us from living comfortably in space and in time.

A heavenly Bridegroom does not have to be touchable to be loved or to be such that one finds one's complete delight in him. It is good that he cannot be understood. Instead of trying to understand him we need to draw nearer and nearer to him, in order to *know* him.

When an electron jumps from the outer shell of an atom to the inner shell, light is emitted. Similarly, whoever does not remain outside the Godhead, but runs to his embraces, becomes an emitter of light. The words of Jesus, 'You are the light of the world', become a reality.

There are some things which are completely absent from the Song. For example, the word 'truth'. Why is this?

When scrutinised, many accepted beliefs are seen to be

inadequate. At best they prove to be partially true – true for the left side of the brain. Our brains are divided in two. Only the left operates logically, and declares what is true and what is not. The right side is as important as the other, but is usually left out in the search for truth. It is irrational, lyrical, prompted by impulse, feeling and emotions. A 'truth' examined only by the left side of the brain cannot be entirely true. It ignores half of reality.

What is normally termed 'truth' brings things to a halt. Therefore Solomon never uses the word. For him, the only thing that comprehends the whole of reality, that unites the two halves of the brain's experience, is love like that between the heavenly Bridegroom and his bride. Only belief in love to the uttermost can pass every test.

Another curious omission from the Song is any mention of good deeds done by the bride. The reason is that – as Kant said – nothing can be called good without some qualification. We all have access to the state of being a chosen bride. Some of us, because of natural disadvantages or the possession of a niggardly nature, lack the power to do good deeds. But even such people can shine like jewels, if they only have ardent love and good will. Fruitfulness would not add to their value, nor fruitlessness diminish it. 'To him that works not, but believes on him that justifies the ungodly, his faith is counted for righteousness' (Romans 4:5). The *Zohar* says, 'Blessed is he that nourishes good thoughts towards his Lord; for, even if he cannot put them into practice, the Holy One takes the will for the deed.' It is not good deeds which qualify you to be a bride of Christ.

This Song shows how right St Augustine was when he said, 'Love – and do what you like,' or St Paul, when he taught, 'Love is the fulfilment of all the law.' When we experience holy, supreme love, the moral law which defers to deeds stands mute in adoration.

One final thing is lacking in Somonon's Song – a

biography of the bride. What is her story? How did she live before becoming a believer? Was she a decent girl or a loose one? What sins had she committed, and how many? Humans have biographies. But she is more than human. She partakes of the divine nature.

Darwin looked in vain for the connecting link between ape and man. But we know the link between the entire creation and the Creator. It is the bride. She is the highest point that creation can reach. She met the One who came down to the lowest level to which Godhead can ever descend, and they united. She is a queen; and she is the servant. She is as tiny as a worm; and she is a god. She is outside the sphere of beings who have biographies.

Most of us are not yet truly human. We are still in an embryonic stage, living in mankind's pre-history. Jesus' teaching, 'You are gods,' sounds oddly in our ears. So we find the nature of the bride hard to grasp. We would enquire about her past; for Jesus, she is simply the bride.

Jesus never gave us his own biography. The evangelists are silent about his life between the ages of twelve and thirty. She does not ask him his life's story. He rewarded her discretion by not asking questions about hers. Today they are Bridegroom and bride. Like the high priest Melchisedec of old, they appear 'having neither beginning of days, nor end of life' (Hebrews 7:3).

Adam must have been created as a man of a certain age. Like him, the bride does not have a past. She and the Bridegroom know only an eternal 'today' of love.

Handel composed his *Messiah* while enraptured, in ecstasy. For twenty-three days, he hardly ate. When he completed the second part with the Hallelujah Chorus, his servant found him sitting at his desk with tears running down his cheeks. He said, 'I saw paradise truly, and the great God himself.' Solomon must have composed the Song in such a state of mind.

Therefore the prayers of the bride are innocent as spring mornings, clear as mountain streams. She does not utter prayers for forgiveness, for they are what sinners need. She has passed beyond this. Christ has finished his work with her. All she can do is sing hymns. Earth and heaven ring with her hallelujahs.

But she does not isolate herself on the peaks. She prefers not to be called a 'saint'. Dorothy Day said, 'That's how people try to dismiss you. If you're a saint you must be impractical and Utopian and nobody has to pay any attention to you.' Brides are in close fellowship with Jesus. But they also seek such fellowship with us.

I must finish with an apology. I could not make words convey what happens between the Bridegroom and the bride, for the same reason that you cannot weigh granite columns in pharmaceutical scales. Solomon could not do it, so I most certainly cannot.

We all retain primitive concepts from our early religious training. When we climb unknown spiritual mountains, to describe the unknown, we use the language of the known. There is nothing else we can do.

It is the same in science. In any chunk of ordinary matter you have 100,000,000,000,000,000,000,000 atoms, made up of who knows how many billions of billions of elementary particles. It is unimaginable and inexpressible. Science therefore uses primitive pictures. It uses models of atoms, though it knows well enough that no atom conforms to the model. Reality puts shivers up one's spine. It cannot even be described.

But for believers, there is a way to know the quality of the relationship between the Bridegroom and the bride. Become a bride yourself; and then you will personally experience that relationship.

But when you become a bride, do not become blind in one eye, seeing only the celestial, without concern for the earthly. Both belong to God. Be a great saint, but be a human saint! Remember that Solomon's Song is only one of many books in the Bible.

≈ References ≈

Chapter 1

1 Reported in *Deutschland Magazine*, July 1978.
2 Jay and Emma Hefley, *By Their Blood*, Mott Media Publishing House.

Chapter 3

1 A. Ratziu, *Stolen Church*.
2 H. Hartfeld, *Faith in Spite of the KGB*. Hartfeld is a former prisoner in Soviet jails.
3 *The Arizonian*, November 1982.
4 Paul Goma, *Gherla*, (Gallimard, France).
5 *Lutheran Witness*, October 1972.

Chapter 4

2 *Orthodox Life*, No 78.

Chapter 6

1 R. Radina, *Testaments from the Death House*.

For correspondence with the author, inquiries and gifts for the underground church, the addresses are:

Christian Mission to the Communist World
POB19
Bromley Kent BR1 1DY
Britain

Jesus to the Communist World
PB2947
Torrance 90509
California
USA

Jesus to the Communist World
PB598 Penrith NSW 2750
Australia

Voice of the Martyrs
POB 476
Agege-Lagos
Nigeria

Jesus to the Communist World
PB38, St. Thomas,
Ontario
Canada

Love in Action
POB 4532
11–31 Green Park
New Delhi
India

Jesus to the Communist World
POB 11-295
Ellerslie
Auckland 5
New Zealand

Christian Mission to the Communist World
POB 1145
Krugersdorp 1740
South Africa